MODERN WORLD NATIONS

MODERN WORLD NATIONS

Bangladesh

Douglas A. Phillips
and
Charles F. Gritzner

Series Editor
Charles F. Gritzner
South Dakota State University

CHELSEA HOUSE
PUBLISHERS
An imprint of Infobase Publishing

Frontispiece: Flag of Bangladesh

Cover: Boat traffic along the Buriganga River, Bangladesh.

Bangladesh

Copyright © 2007 by Infobase Publishing

Chelsea House
An imprint of Infobase Publishing
132 West 31st Street
New York NY 10001

ISBN-10: 0-7910-9251-8
ISBN-13: 978-0-7910-9251-4

Library of Congress Cataloging-in-Publication Data
Phillips, Douglas A.
 Bangladesh / Douglas A. Phillips and Charles F. Gritzner.
   p. cm.—(Modern world nations)
 Includes bibliographical references and index.
 ISBN 0-7910-9251-8 (hardcover)
 1. Bangladesh. I. Gritzner, Charles F. II. Title. III. Series.
 DS393.4.P45 2007
 954.92—dc22   2006032006

Chelsea House books are available at special discounts when purchased in bulk quantities for businesses, associations, institutions, or sales promotions. Please call our Special Sales Department in New York at (212) 967-8800 or (800) 322-8755.

You can find Chelsea House on the World Wide Web at http://www.chelseahouse.com

Series and Cover design by Takeshi Takahashi

Printed in the United States of America

Bang Hermitage 10 9 8 7 6 5 4 3 2 1

This book is printed on acid-free paper.

All links, Web addresses, and Internet search terms were checked and verified to be correct at the time of publication. Because of the dynamic nature of the Web, some addresses and links may have changed since publication and may no longer be valid.

Table of Contents

MODERN WORLD NATIONS

Bangladesh

CHAPTER

1

Introducing Bangladesh

In exploring the world, people often talk about places they would like to travel. Countries such as France, the United Kingdom, Germany, Japan, Australia, and New Zealand often appear at the top of such lists. Few people, however, would ever include the fascinating country of Bangladesh on such a list! Why? Often, people's feelings about a country are tainted with negative images from the past that aren't necessarily representative of the present. This may be part of the case with Bangladesh. Many images of the country are negative. The country's brutal war for liberation in 1972 may linger in the memory of some. For others, visions of the devastation, famine, and death caused by the hurricane in 1974 may come to mind. (The term *cyclone* is also used for a hurricane in this part of the world and will be used throughout the book.) Grinding poverty and spiraling overpopulation combine to create a negative image that keeps most people from thinking of Bangladesh as a dream vacation destination.

Who, after all, would want to spend a holiday in a country that ranks near the very bottom of the Human Development Index and dead last among the world's countries in terms of rampant corruption? And if the foregoing deterrents were not enough, more than half of the country's total land area frequently disappears beneath churning floodwaters!

The foregoing description presents only one side of this fascinating country's personality. To a geographer, few places on Earth hold more interest. A contrasting view of Bangladesh sees the country as a land celebrating the early stages of democracy, with people and a culture that are extremely interesting and welcoming. Contrasting views of Bangladesh can even be found in music. A local view is presented by the words of the national anthem of Bangladesh:

My Bengal of gold (Precious),
I love you
Forever your skies,
Your air set my heart in tune
As if it were a flute.

In spring, Oh mother mine,
The fragrance from your mango groves
Makes me wild with joy,
Ah, what a thrill!
In autumn, Oh mother mine,
In the full blossomed paddy fields,
I have seen spread all over sweet smiles!

Ah, what a beauty, what shades,
What an affection
and what a tenderness!
What a quilt have you spread
At the feet of banyan trees
And along the banks of rivers!

Oh mother mine, words from your lips
Are like nectar to my ears!
Ah, what a thrill!
If sadness, Oh mother mine,
Casts a gloom on your face,
My eyes are filled with tears!

The anthem clearly expresses the obvious love that Bangladeshis have for their country. In their eyes, it is "of gold" with a beauty that the Bangladeshis appreciate. In contrast, consider the song "Bangla Desh," written by George Harrison of the Beatles and featured in the album called *Concert for Bangladesh* (1972). Harrison wrote the song in response to the suffering endured by Bengali refugees who were driven from East Pakistan (which became Bangladesh after the war) by West Pakistani forces during the Bangladeshi Liberation War in 1971. The words are markedly different from the national anthem and recount the "disaster" and "distress" of the war as seen through the eyes of a resident of Bangladesh. The song was written shortly before the Concert For Bangla Desh, which Harrison organized after Pakistani musician Ravi Shankar informed him of the gravity of the situation. Held on August 1 of that year in New York City's Madison Square Garden, the charity event raised well over $200,000, which was then donated to UNICEF to aid the homeless refugees of East Pakistan.

The contrasting words in the two songs are starkly different. Which best describes the real Bangladesh? Is the answer to this question neither, or is it perhaps both? That is a question that this book will attempt to answer. Our journey to gain an understanding of Bangladesh will be a difficult and complex trip. But it is an important one to make, as we seek to more closely examine this small but densely populated nation located on the Indian subcontinent, the peninsula landmass of the continent of Asia.

As you visit Bangladesh through the pages of this book, you will want to keep in mind six very important "R's" that constitute the foundation of its physical and human geography: rain, rivers, rice, rural, religion, and revolution. The seasonal distribution of rain and the importance of the country's three huge rivers are fundamental to understanding the country's physical geography. Its huge population is supported by rice, the leading food crop that is both nutritious and high yielding. Most Bangladeshis are rural, with a culture best described as being traditional and "folk." Religion has played a very important role in the country's history and continues to be a very important aspect of Bangladeshi culture today. Finally, the country has experienced several major political revolutions on its pathway to independence.

Bangladesh is a small country that is only 55,599 square miles (144,000 square kilometers), an area slightly smaller than the state of Iowa or Wisconsin. Amazingly, nearly 150 million people—fully one-half the population of the United States, or about five times as many people as live in all of Canada—are packed into this small territory! Needless to say, this condition creates one of the world's highest population densities, a whopping 2,600 people per square mile (about 1,000 per square kilometer). The government of Bangladesh believes that the population is too high and has worked to address this situation. With a 2 percent annual rate of natural population increase, the situation is much better than in times past. Three decades ago, the birthrate was nearly twice as high. In 1970, the average woman would give birth to about six children; today, the figure has dropped to three.

Bangladesh is located on the Bay of Bengal and is only bordered by two countries, India and Myanmar. It formerly was a part of India and later Pakistan, but the country gained independence in 1971 after a chaotic split from West Pakistan. Politics and religion have frequently served to force millions of refugees to flee from one area to another. This first occurred when dominantly Muslim Pakistan split from primarily Hindu India. Then it happened again when East and West Pakistan split to become Pakistan and Bangladesh. The country's turbulent

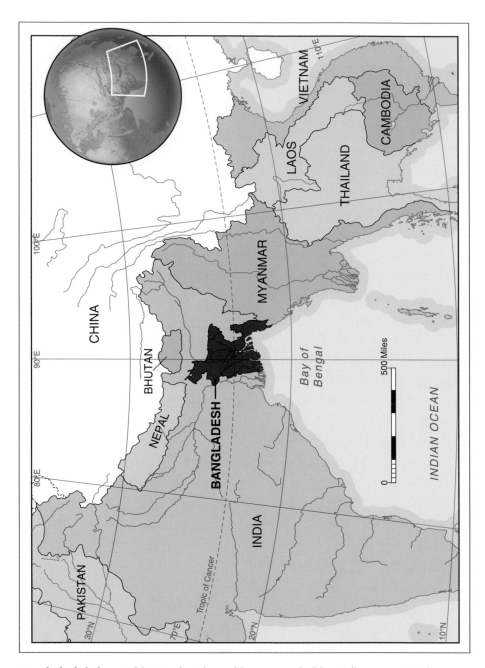

Bangladesh is located in South Asia and is surrounded by India, except to the south, where it is bordered by the Bay of Bengal, and in the extreme southeast, where the country of Myanmar borders it. Although Bangladesh is only about the size of the state of Iowa, it is home to nearly 150 million people.

past, environmental hardships, and huge population have combined to leave the country impoverished.

The tsunami that struck Bangladesh and many other Asian
and African nations in December 2004 is only one of the environmental challenges that Bangladesh currently faces. Fortunately,
few deaths resulted from the tsunami in Bangladesh. But the same
summer monsoon rains that result in bumper crops also can cause
devastating flooding that places much of the country under water.
(Monsoon is a seasonal shift of winds that typically brings rain to
Bangladesh and other South Asian countries.) With most farmers
and others living on low, flood-vulnerable lands, the effects of
monsoons can be devastating. The United Nations Environment
Programme (UNEP) estimates that 80 million Bangladeshis are in
danger from the effects of flooding. If Earth's climate continues to
warm and sea levels rise, the country's susceptibility to flooding
will become much worse. Compounding the problem are the diseases that thrive under conditions of polluted water and increased
mosquito populations that also depend upon surface water.
Malaria, dengue fever, bacterial diarrhea, hepatitis, typhoid fever,
and leptospirosis are just some of the diseases that are widespread
among the country's population.

Cyclones are another natural hazard that can impact the
land and people of Bangladesh. Tropical cyclones form over the
southern end of the Bay of Bengal during summer and fall and
then move northward toward the coast of Bangladesh, causing
severe flooding and frequent tidal surges that affect the low-
lying lands.

Human habitation also poses a number of threats to the
environment of this nation. Among these are water pollution,
deforestation, water shortages (during the country's dry season, there is too little water), soil degradation, and a number of
additional problems caused by overpopulation and poverty.

Bangladesh is also an Islamic nation, with the fourth-largest
Muslim population in the world. Islam was brought to the country by Turks from Central Asia. Since its introduction many

Bangladesh has the world's fourth-largest Muslim population, which translates to approximately 83 percent of its residents. Pictured here are Muslim devotees traveling to the annual Biswa Ijtema, or World Congregation of Islamic Preachers, in the town of Tongi, which is on the banks of the Turag River. The Biswa Ijtema is the world's second-largest Muslim gathering (behind the Hajj pilgrimage in Mecca, Saudi Arabia).

centuries ago, the faith has flourished to the degree that today 83 percent of the population is Muslim. Reflecting the country's past lineage, Hindus make up 16 percent of the population. Because of the country's dominant Islamic population, there has been occasional support for radical Islamic efforts around the world. Most of the population has not been radicalized, however, and support for such activities has been very moderate.

This moderate tone may be changing because so many Bangladeshi laborers are employed in Saudi Arabia and elsewhere in the Middle East. They become easy targets for recruitment by terrorist and other radical groups. Also, Jagrata Muslim Janata Bangladesh (JMJB) is a militant Islamic group operating in Bangladesh that has goals similar to those of al-Qaeda. The name JMJB translates into Awakened Muslim Masses of Bangladesh. Presently, the group is focused on terrorist activities such as bombings in Bangladesh, India, and Myanmar. They primarily recruit poor and disillusioned young people to their ranks. The government is working to suppress JMJB and reduce radical Islam, but the government itself is poor, weak, and largely ineffective because of widespread problems of political corruption. For five years in a row, Transparency International, a worldwide organization that exposes governmental corruption, has named Bangladesh as the most corrupt country in the world.

Fighting radical Islam in Bangladesh will most likely require outside help. The country is simply too poor to take on the militants in their own land and too divided, with two political parties at extreme odds with each other. These elements, combined with a history filled with lawlessness, may threaten the very foundation of the country's political system. Unaided and unprotected, moderate Islam may be threatened in the coming years by the rising radical militant elements. Were this to happen, the Bangladeshis' struggle to become a stable democracy could be crushed.

Which song best reflects Bangladesh? Is it the words of the national anthem or the song "Bangla Desh" by George Harrison? We have only begun our journey into exploring this troubled, complex, and fascinating country. Read on and decide for yourself!

CHAPTER

2

Physical Landscapes

Nature has been both kind and ruthlessly cruel to Bangladesh. The relatively tiny country is sandwiched between three barriers. To the north is the world's highest mountain range, the towering Himalayas. To the east are rugged mountains and dense forests through which no major transportation artery passes. Only to the west is the land relatively open—it provides a doorway to India, with which the Bangladeshis have had a strained relationship since gaining independence in 1971. Most of the country lies within a zone of very mild tropical climate.

Rainfall is abundant, with most of the country receiving more than 80 inches (200 centimeters) of precipitation annually. Unfortunately, the climate is highly seasonal, with a relatively dry winter and torrential rainfall during the summer monsoon season. During roughly half the year, drought poses a problem; during the other half, the country is subject to severe flooding.

Much like the state of Louisiana, Bangladesh's landscape is tied to the water. Three large rivers, the Ganges (Ganga), Jamuna (the name given the Brahmaputra River when it flows from India into Bangladesh), and the Meghna flow through the country. Nearly the entire country is formed by rich *alluvium* (stream-deposited soil) that ranks among the world's most fertile soils. Unfortunately, the same rivers that have created most of the country's land and given it the soil needed to produce food for its huge population also contribute to some of the world's most devastating floods. It is doubtful whether any country other than the Netherlands has a lower average elevation or is more vulnerable to flooding than Bangladesh. To the south, the Bay of Bengal offers the country a window to the global sea. But silt deposited by the combined rivers makes navigation difficult. Further, occasional cyclones send walls of saltwater surging over thousands of square miles of low-lying farmland. When this happens, all crops, habitation, livestock, and even human population can be swept away. The salt left behind in the soil in the wake of cyclones makes the soil useless for farming until rain eventually washes the salts away.

In Bangladesh, it is very difficult to speak of a "natural" environment. Nearly every aspect of nature has been altered by human activity over thousands of years. Natural flora has been replaced by crops and natural fauna by livestock and poultry. Various engineering works have been constructed in an attempt to protect the country's settlements, fields, and other elements of the cultural (man-made) landscape. In fact, few places on Earth show a greater impact of the human imprint upon the land than does Bangladesh. In the remainder of this chapter, you will learn about the country's landform features, its weather and climate, its weather-related natural hazards, and its plant and animal life.

LANDFORM FEATURES
Nearly all of Bangladesh (roughly 80 percent) is a very flat alluvial plain that has built up gradually over hundreds of thousands

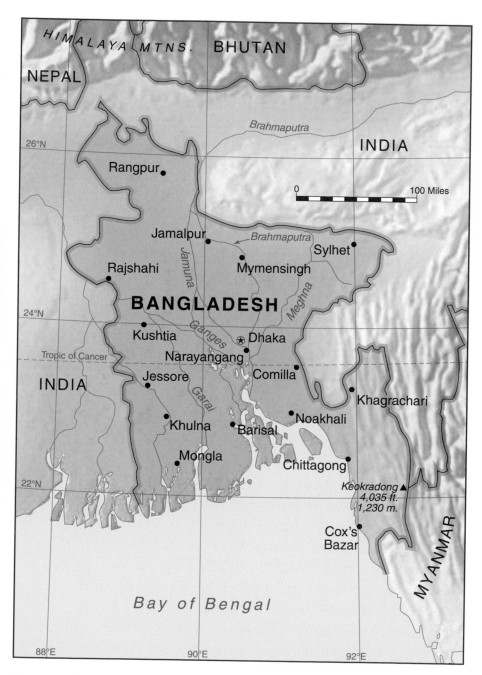

Approximately 80 percent of Bangladesh is flat alluvial plain, the majority of which is less than 10 meters (32 feet) above sea level. The exception is the Chittagong Hills, which rise to approximately 4,000 feet (1,219 meters) and are located in the southeastern part of the country, near Myanmar.

of years from silt deposited by the three rivers that flow into and across the country. Only the Chittagong Hills, located in the far southeast corner of the country, break the monotony of otherwise quite featureless terrain. Even there, near Keokradong, the elevation only rises to about 4,000 feet (1,219 meters).

Much of the country's territory is situated on river deltas. The Ganges, Jamuna, and Meghna rivers join near the center of the country. Downstream from the capital of Dhaka, the combined streams break into many distributaries (deltaic channels) that flow into the Bay of Bengal. This very low-lying depositional plain area goes by several names, including the Lower Gangetic Plain, the Mouths of the Ganges, and the Sundarbans. Because the land is flat and also composed of fertile alluvium, about two-thirds of the country is suitable for farming or grazing. So why is only a small part of the land—about 6 percent—farmed or grazed? This seems strange for a country with so many people and such a desperate need for food and export products. The answer may surprise you. Each summer, much of the land disappears beneath floodwaters, and dry land is so scarce that nearly all of it is settled—it is occupied by people and houses, rather than by crops and livestock.

WEATHER AND CLIMATE

Most of Bangladesh experiences a seasonally wet and dry tropical (in the south and east) and subtropical (in the west and north) climate. Temperatures are warm throughout the year. Summers are very hot and muggy, averaging about 80°F (27°C). Unlike most of the world, however, the hottest month is April—just before the cooling (but drenching) monsoons arrive. Summer afternoon temperatures typically climb into the low to mid-90s°F (33 to 35°C) with record highs hovering around 110 to 112°F (44°C). Because of the high humidity, however, a typical summer afternoon will actually feel like a scorching (and dripping!) 115 to 120°F (46 to 49°C). Winters are mild, with temperatures averaging in the 60s°F (16 to

22°C). January is the coldest month. Conditions are very similar to those experienced in southern Florida during the winter, with frost being very rare.

Four primary factors combine to create the weather (the day-to-day conditions of the atmosphere) and climate (the long-term average conditions of the weather): the country's latitudinal position, compact area, low elevation, and abundance of water. The country's latitudinal position accounts for its tropical temperatures. Located between roughly 21 and 26 degrees north, Bangladesh is the same distance from the equator as southern Florida, the Bahamas, and the northern Caribbean islands. The fact that nearly the entire country experiences similar temperatures is accounted for by its compact area and uniformly low elevation. An abundance of water also helps account for the lack of temperature extremes (water surfaces help to moderate temperatures).

What sets Bangladesh and much of the remainder of South Asia apart from the rest of the world is its unique pattern of winds and precipitation—the monsoons. As mentioned previously, some areas of Bangladesh receive well over 80 inches (200 centimeters) of rain per year. However, some areas in the northeastern part of the country receive twice that amount. Even the drier western portion of Bangladesh receives more than 60 inches (152 centimeters) of precipitation each year. (By comparison, in Louisiana, the wettest U.S. state, the average annual rainfall is about 55 inches, or 140 centimeters.)

Heavy rainfall is typical of Bangladesh. Yet drought is a major concern each year for many residents. How can this be? The answer lies in the nature of the monsoons and the seasonal patterns of precipitation that result from these winds. (The word *monsoon* means season.) In fact, more than three-fourths of all rain falls during a four-month monsoon season. During the winter months, winds are from the north, blowing southward from a high-pressure system located in eastern Siberia. These winds are very dry. During the summer, usually

Bangladesh's warm tropical climate and low-lying terrain make it conducive to frequent flooding. Pictured here are rickshaw pullers who are attempting to make their way through the flooded streets of Dhaka, the capital of Bangladesh, after several days of monsoon rain in September 2004.

beginning in June and ending in early autumn, the winds reverse. They blow from a high-pressure system over the Indian Ocean northward to an area of low pressure located over Southwest Asia. As the winds sweep across the tropical waters of the equatorial Indian Ocean, they pick up huge amounts of moisture. It is this moisture that drenches Bangladesh during the monsoon season.

WEATHER-RELATED NATURAL HAZARDS

Bangladesh is one of the world's most disaster-prone countries. Few places have been more ravaged more frequently or by a greater variety of environmental hazards. Nearly every year, floods, cyclones, storm surges (high water, much like a very high tide pushed ashore by storm winds), and even tornadoes take a huge toll on life and property.

Floods

In Bangladesh, no environmental hazard can match flooding in terms of devastation. The country's relatively flat, low-lying terrain makes it extremely vulnerable to rising water. In fact, roughly two-thirds of the entire land area is subject to severe flooding on a fairly regular basis. First, the summer monsoons bring drenching rain that floods wide areas of the country on an annual basis. Second, the drainage basins of the three rivers that flow into the country drain some of the world's wettest areas. Rain that falls over an area of roughly 1 million square miles (2.6 million square kilometers) is funneled into Bangladesh. To make matters worse, a relatively short four-month rainy season and a long winter drought ensures that the water arrives all at once rather than being spread out over an entire year. For several decades, scientists believed that widespread deforestation occurring on the slopes of the Himalayas was responsible for increased flooding. They reasoned that in the absence of forest cover, rainwater would collect and run off much faster. Recent research, however, suggests that this is not the case. Evidently, little change has occurred in the amount of water carried by the rivers over the years. What has changed is that Bangladesh's population has increased. People have been forced to move into flood-prone areas; hence, the destruction has increased dramatically. (A similar situation has occurred along the hurricane-prone southeastern U.S. coastal region.)

You may have heard the phrase that places someone faced with bad luck as being "between a rock and a hard place." This certainly applies to Bangladesh, except rather than being located between solid materials, it is between quite different sources of floodwater. As you have seen, some damage comes from rain that falls within the country itself. Some is transported into Bangladesh by the three large rivers that enter from beyond its borders. The third source of floodwater is the Bay of Bengal. The bay itself is shaped somewhat like a funnel. As water is forced northward by strong winds, it is compressed by less space and hence rises. Storm surges of windblown water as high as 20 feet deep can wash ashore. When this happens, death and destruction can occur on a massive scale. In 1970, for example, an estimated 500,000 to 1 million people lost their lives in the coastal region. Several geographers who were in the area at the time were shocked and horrified by the level of death and destruction.

Bangladesh is never far removed from disaster. In 1985, winds approaching 100 miles (160 kilometers) per hour sent a 13-foot (4-meter)-high wall of water surging across low-lying coastal islands and the adjacent mainland. The water rushed upstream, jumping riverbanks and flowing across fields and villages. When it was over, more than 11,000 people had died, nearly 100,000 houses had been destroyed, and an estimated 135,000 head of livestock were killed. In 1991, another cyclone struck the southeast coastal region with even more devastating results that resulted in the loss of 125,000 to 150,000 lives. As people flock to the coastal region to settle new islands and mud flats, surely the deadly toll will continue to climb.

With the exception of the Netherlands and a number of low-lying islands scattered around the world's oceans, no country faces a greater threat from possible sea level rise. During recent decades, the threat of global warming has received widespread attention from scientists and the media. Many reputable scientists believe that the earth's atmosphere is warming, as a result of increased amounts of gases such as CO_2 released by the burning of fossil fuels. Others say that the earth is simply in a natural warming cycle. Regardless of the reasons or causes, if the planet does continue to warm and the sea level rises, much of Bangladesh will be vulnerable to encroaching seawater. Low-lying coastal land will sink

In April 1991, one of the worst cyclones in Bangladesh's history struck the southeastern part of the country with 155 mile-per-hour winds and a 20-foot (6-meter) storm surge. The devastating storm killed at least 138,000 people and left nearly 10 million homeless, including these residents of Urir Island in the Bay of Bengal.

beneath the sea, and salt water will reach inland rendering freshwater supplies unusable.

Storms

The devastating coastal storm surges that are described above result from tropical cyclones. On average, about 16 cyclones roar up the Bay of Bengal and strike Bangladesh each decade, or between one and two per year. Winds can exceed 100 miles per hour and destroy structures, trees, crops, and most everything else in their path. The drenching rains that accompany the storms often cause severe flooding. The greatest destruction in a rather limited area, however, comes from the accompanying storm surge. It is this phenomenon that takes the greatest toll of life and inflicts the greatest damage to property.

When you think of tornadoes, what may first come to mind is the "Tornado Alley" of the United States, an area that includes parts of Texas, Oklahoma, Kansas, and Nebraska. In fact, more than 90 percent of all tornadoes ever recorded have occurred in the United States. These vicious storms normally occur when there is a clash between warm and moist air and cool and dry air—conditions that certainly are rare in Bangladesh. Tornadoes do occur in Bangladesh, however, and in 1989, a deadly tornado struck near Dhaka in the central part of the country and killed an estimated 1,300 people. Amazingly, this is twice the number of people to have died in the most deadly tornado ever to strike the United States!

Drought

It may seem strange to suggest that drought, or a seasonal lack of water, also poses a threat to many Bangladeshis. Most of the country does have adequate stream and ground water (although much of both may be highly polluted). The drought problem stems from two factors: the seasonality of precipitation and the distribution of settlement. The wet monsoon season lasts for approximately four months, during which as much as 80 percent of the annual precipitation is received. The remaining eight months of the year (October through May) are relatively dry. Small streams dry up and disappear, shallow wells go dry, and fields become parched. Bangladesh and most of its people are very poor. They cannot afford elaborate water-diversion projects. Because of the very flat terrain, it is not possible in most places to build dams that would store water in reservoirs. A second problem involves where people live. Because of river flooding, many people live on *interfluves*, the higher ground located between rivers. Because of their location, they do not have ready access to stream water.

ECOSYSTEMS

Technically speaking, an ecosystem includes the interaction of *all* natural elements as they affect plant and animal life. A major influence, as you would expect, is weather and climate. Landforms and water features also play an important role. Temperatures and exposure to the sun (influencing evaporation from the soil and the surface of water, and transpiration, the release of moisture through the leaves of plants) influence plant life and animal habitat, but in Bangladesh, these elements play only a minor role. Climate is relatively similar throughout the entire country—hot and wet, with a marked seasonal distribution of precipitation to which plants must adapt. Elevation, too, is fairly constant throughout the country.

A map of potential natural vegetation shows that most of Bangladesh falls within two vegetative zones: tropical rain forest in the southern deltaic area of the country and semi-deciduous mixed forest elsewhere. In a country with such a high population density, however, these distinctions are all but meaningless. Humans have altered the natural vegetative landscape for millennia, resulting in very little "natural" vegetation or original animal life habitat. In fact, only in the more remote upland areas and coastal rain forest zone do even small parcels of land have patches of natural woodlands where some wildlife can be found. Insects, birds, fish, and reptiles (some of which are deadly poisonous) are found everywhere. Of the larger wild animals, the best known is the famous Bengal tiger, found mainly in the coastal rain forest region. Unfortunately, these magnificent animals are being threatened with extinction as their habitat is penetrated and destroyed by the country's burgeoning population.

There are few places in the world where people are more dependent upon nature's offerings, more susceptible to nature's forces, or have altered nature to a greater degree than in Bangladesh.

3

Bangladesh Through Time

Historical geography is a marvelous treasure. It chronicles the stories, traditions, beliefs, customs, people, legends, and events that shape the world we see today. It provides a glimpse at the legacy of a people and country that helps us better understand why the country is as it is. It ties people not only to the land they occupy, but to one another as cultures evolve, interact, and often clash. Bangladesh is no exception to this pattern. The past of Bangladesh is filled with turmoil and tragedy, pitfalls and promises. These journeys have shaped the country's people and help them to face the challenges provided in the twenty-first century. At the same time, past events can taint the attitudes of people in the present with prejudices and often false images of the past. What does the historical geography of Bangladesh tell us? How do past events impact the present? These and other questions will be addressed in this brief chronicle of Bangladesh's past.

Bangladesh has a very short political history as an independent country. The country gained independence from West Pakistan on March 26, 1971. The Bangladeshis refer to the struggle against West Pakistan as the Liberation War of Bangladesh. But the birth of this poor nation was tumultuous and fraught with sacrifice and loss as people struggled to create their democratic vision for a new country. Even with its short history as an independent state, Bangladesh has a long history preceding this nationhood that includes colonial rulers, time as a part of India, time as a part of Pakistan, and a bloody and disruptive civil war. All of these elements and others make up the chronicles of Bangladesh.

THE FIRST PEOPLE OF BANGLADESH

It is not known when the first humans set foot in what is now Bangladesh. Scientists believe the human species originated in equatorial East Africa. There is evidence of a human presence in Southeast and East Asia hundreds of thousands of years ago. Almost certainly the route of these early migrants would have taken them south of the Himalayas through present-day Bangladesh. No trace has been found of this early journey, so we can only speculate on whether and when it occurred.

The first civilization in Bangladesh can be traced to about 3,000 years ago; however, early archaeological and historical records are sparse and sketchy. Thus, this account of the early historical geography of settlement and culture will have some gaps, because information was not well recorded before the rise of the Gupta Empire (in the fourth century A.D.), one of the largest political and military empires in ancient India. Historical records improved greatly under the Guptas, who not only recorded historical events but also related history in the literature that exists from this time period.

Preceding the Gupta Empire were the Dravidians, who were the first people to arrive into the area we now call Bangladesh. They came from the areas of the Indus River and northwestern India about 1000 B.C. These Dravidian-speaking people were later called Bang, and other tribes in the area had names such as Banga, Bangala, Bangal, Vanga, and Bengal. These names served as the linguistic roots for the regions later called Bengal and Bangladesh. The area known as Bengal would roughly include the areas of Bangladesh and the Indian state of West Bengal. Following in the footsteps of Dravidians, Indo-Aryans began to arrive from India during the fifth and sixth centuries B.C.

The first homegrown civilization that rose to power was the Mauryan Empire, which was founded by Chandragupta Maurya, who reigned from 321–296 B.C. He was born to a destitute family. As a youth, he was sent into exile by the king and others in the court. During this time of exile, he met Alexander the Great, who was attempting to invade India. Even though Alexander failed in his attempt to conquer India, he encouraged Maurya to take the Kingdom of Magadha and India. After Alexander's death, there was a power vacuum. Maurya proceeded to conquer the Punjab region of northern India. He then also conquered the Kingdom of Magadha in northern India, where he killed the king and his family. Maurya then extended his kingdom from the Arabian Sea eastward to the Bay of Bengal. He died in 296 B.C., but his empire stretched over most of the areas today known as India, Bangladesh, and Pakistan. His dynasty existed from 321 to 180 B.C.

Ashoka (273–232 B.C.) is considered the most famous Mauryan emperor, as well as the greatest leader of ancient India. He was a brilliant military commander and extended the Mauryan Empire even farther. A war with the Kalinga forces in east-central India resulted in hundreds of thousands of deaths at the hand of Ashoka's army. Upon seeing the large-scale devastation and death, Ashoka was shocked and remorseful. He became opposed to warfare and adopted the peaceful beliefs of Buddhism as his philosophy. Thus, under Ashoka's rule during the Mauryan Empire, Buddhism spread rapidly across India and

The Mauryan Empire ruled India, including the region that is today Bangladesh, from 322 to 183 B.C. One of the most powerful kings of the empire was Ashoka, who reigned from 273 to 232 B.C., and built several monuments to honor the peaceful beliefs of Buddhism. Pictured here is the temple at Bodh Gaya, which was built by Ashoka and is located just to the west of Bangladesh in the state of Bihar.

into the area of Bengal. Ashoka not only renounced war and fighting, but also banned hunting and forced labor. Instead of war, he initiated the building of public works and established goodwill with other countries in the region. This resulted in the empire having 40 years of prosperity and peace. For this,

Ashoka is remembered as being one of the Indian subcontinent's greatest leaders.

Soon after Ashoka, the Mauryan Empire declined, and the eastern area of Bengal became the state of Samatata, which existed from A.D. 319 to 540. Samatata included many areas in present-day Bangladesh. During that time, the region was ruled by the Gupta Empire. Although politically independent, Samatata still had ties and was subservient to the Gupta Dynasty in India. Buddhism flourished in Samatata. During this period, a Chinese pilgrim named Sheng Chi visited Samatata's capital city of Bangrastra. In his writings, he described that as many as 4,000 monks lived in Samatata, where Buddhism had became the favored philosophy during that era.

The years of the Gupta Empire are often called the golden age of India. The first Gupta king was Chandragupta I (reigned A.D. 319–335). He rapidly expanded the kingdom by marriage and military means. Chandragupta I was the first of the Guptas to be referred to as "Maharajadhiraja," which means king of kings. Upon his death, his son Samudragupta (reigned A.D. 335–380) assumed the throne. He was perhaps the greatest of the Gupta kings, because he is credited with the unification of India. He also is considered the father of the Gupta monetary system, which consisted of gold coins named Dinera, like the Roman coins after which they were modeled. Samudragupta strongly supported cultural work in the arts, religion, language, and literature. Even though he was a Hindu who worshipped Vishnu, Samudragupta was very tolerant of other religions such as Buddhism. Because of this tolerance, during the Gupta era, Buddhism reached its zenith in India.

Samudragupta's son Chandragupta II succeeded him to the throne in 380 and ruled until A.D. 413. It was during the reign of the second Chandragupta that India reached the peak of its wealth and opulence. Chandragupta II was the grandson of Chandragupta I. He was from a different family lineage than Chandragupta Maurya of the earlier Mauryan Empire, which was located in eastern India in the area that includes much of present-day Bangladesh.

The end of the Gupta Empire came with the invasion by the Hephthalites, or White Huns. The Huns (called Hunas), were a confederation of tribes that came from Central Asia and attacked from the northwest. Huna king Toramana broke through the Gupta military lines in 480, and by 500, the Hephthalites had conquered most of the Gupta Empire. The empire then fragmented into smaller kingdoms with a smaller version of the Gupta kingdom lingering for a few decades. Later, in the 530s, the Hunas were collectively pushed out of the area by the smaller Gupta kingdom in alliance with other smaller kingdoms. The lineage of the main Gupta family line remained until the last Gupta king, Vishnugupta, who ruled from 540 to 550. A distant line of the Gupta family continued to rule Magadha, located in eastern India or current-day Bangladesh, until they were overpowered by Vardhana King Harsha in the seventh century.

The first independent Bengal king was Shashanka, who was king of Gauda, which was located in eastern Bengal along the coast. Shashanka extended the lands of Gauda and ruled from the capital city of Karnasuvarna. Upon Shashanka's death in 670, there was little central control, and anarchy prevailed in the region for a long period of time.

In 750, Gopala became king of the region. Some say he was elected by the people to bring an end to the chaos and disunity, whereas others say he gained control by currying favor with influential people. In any case, as king, he soon added the Vanga region to his kingdom, and a new golden age dawned for Bengal. Gopala was a Buddhist and built a temple at Nalanda (an ancient city in today's Bihar state in eastern India adjacent to Bangladesh) along with developing many religious schools. Gopala's kingdom ushered in the start of the Pala Dynasty, which lasted four centuries until 1150. This era was important in that it provided political stability for the region, which previously had been marked by confusion and chaos. The Palas also continued the tradition of religious tolerance, because the kings following Gopala were mostly Hindu. New forms of religion merged thinking of Buddhists and Hindus and created Tantric cults, which adopted beliefs from both religions. Literature, poetry, architecture, and terra cotta artwork also flourished during the Pala era.

The flowering of the Pala era was crushed when Hindu Senas came to rule. Under the leadership of Vijayasena, the Senas started their rise to power in 1097, in the southern Indian state of Karnataka. Vijayasena gradually gained control of most of Bengal and pushed the Pala Dynasty out of existence around 1150. Vijayasena was an orthodox Hindu who did not tolerate Buddhism and other faiths, and stressed strict adherence to Hindu caste customs and teachings. This lack of tolerance greatly weakened the influence of the Buddhists in Bengal. Vijayasena was a good administrator and he advocated peace and prosperity during his reign. This stands in contrast to the occasional brutality he showed with his lack of tolerance toward Buddhism. Sanskrit language and literature flourished during the Sena era, but the dynasty started to disintegrate by 1205. Smaller and more vulnerable kingdoms were established in Bengal, but another conqueror loomed on the horizon.

THE RISE OF ISLAM

At the dawn of the thirteenth century, an ominous dark cloud hung over the region to the west of Bengal. By 1201, powerful Turks were moving eastward across India with the goal of taking control of Bengal to spread the Islamic faith and gain control of the region's vast wealth. Turks had been gaining strength since they began acquiring territory in India in 1175. Under pressure from the Turks, Lakhmanasena, the last of the Sena kings, fled to Vanga (East Bengal) in 1204 and briefly established his capital in the city of Vikrampur before his death. However, Lakhmanasena died without an heir, and the Sena Dynasty became vulnerable to the Turks. In addition, Buddhists who were persecuted under Sena kings were not inclined to protect the Sena Dynasty. Thus they quickly embraced the new invaders and the new religion, and the Sena Dynasty collapsed.

The Turks who took control of Bengal were not from Turkey; rather, they were from Turkmenistan in Central Asia. Eighty years of Turkish rule followed Lakhmanasena's death in 1204. This era was marked by infighting among Turk generals, during which time twelve different *sultans* (Turkish leaders) ruled in the first 50 years. Five of these sultans were killed by other Turks. After this era of political turmoil and transition, leaders began to rule for longer periods of time.

In 1227, the Turk leadership in Bengal was forced to accept subjugation to the Delhi Sultanate in India, which had been established in 1206. However, in 1341, Bengal became independent of Delhi. Dhaka, the present-day capital of Bangladesh, was established as the seat of government for the Bengal region. The Turks continued to rule Bengal until Akbar the Great conquered Dhaka in 1576. Akbar came to power in 1556 at the age of 13. During his reign, he greatly expanded the Mughal Empire, which had been established in 1526 by Babar. Babar was Akbar's grandfather and a descendent of Genghis Khan. The Mughal Empire lasted until 1757, but during their reign they kept Bengal as a province until the British took control.

By the time Akbar died in 1605, his empire stretched from Afghanistan in the west to Orissa in east India. Akbar was a tolerant leader who attempted to blend together the best elements of Islam, Hinduism, Christianity, and other religions into a new religion called Din-i-Ilahi, which means Divine Faith. Even though the effort ultimately failed, historians reflect favorably upon his religious experiment. Akbar was an effective administrator who extended trade and economic development across the empire. Architecture built during Akbar's reign, like the Red Fort in Delhi, still exists today, and his legacy is deeply imprinted upon the culture and landscape of India and Bangladesh.

Under Akbar the Great, who ruled the Mughal Empire from 1556 to 1605, Bengal became an important agricultural center, as well as an important hub for trade. Akbar is depicted in this seventeenth-century painting atop an elephant.

After Akbar, Bengal gained more autonomy than other provinces, because it was a long distance away from the central government in Delhi. Nevertheless, there was still a strong development of culture, including the economy, during the Mughal rule in Bengal. Bridges and roads were built along with palaces. Agriculture became very important as the Bengal region served as a breadbasket for India. Dhaka grew increasingly important as an economic center, and new trade routes were developed. Even though political control was far away in Delhi, East India—the present area of Bangladesh and West Bengal was moving forward.

EUROPEANS COME TO THE BENGAL REGION

Europeans had long-standing interests in India and the Indian subcontinent. The Portuguese, Dutch, British, Danish, and French all were engaged in the region. Frequently, they battled against one another to gain influence and control. The British prevailed in the struggle to colonize the subcontinent, but the other European powers continued to hold islands of control in the region. The attraction for these powers was the potential for gaining riches, markets, influence, and colonies.

While each of the European countries left a mark on Bengal, the British prevailed and made the largest imprint upon the region. Early British interests in India were managed by the British East India Company, which Queen Elizabeth I established in 1600 by a charter. The company was funded by stockholders who sought to make money from trade with India. The charter granted by Elizabeth I gave the company a very favorable monopoly over trade with India for a period of 21 years. Strangely, the strength of the company grew and eventually it became the virtual ruler of India. Its power was so great that it controlled not only the government, but also trade and the military. Surprisingly, competition for the lucrative Indian trade also came from England rather than other nations. The monopoly was so powerful and wealthy that the British Parliament allowed the formation of a second stockholder company in 1698 to trade with India. The new company was named the English Trading Company to the East Indies. Some of the stockholders in the new company also held a stake in the well-positioned British East India Company. Nonetheless, quarrels broke out between the two companies until they finally merged in 1702.

The British stronghold in East India and Bengal was established in Calcutta. Fort William, named after King William I, was built by the British East India Company in Calcutta in 1699. The city would later serve as the British administrative headquarters for the region. The city grew rapidly with the British trade, and the political interference of the British also increased in the region. In 1717, Mughal emperor Farrukhsiyar exempted the British from duties on trading in Bengal for the paltry sum of 3,000 Rupees. This upset the ruling family in Bengal and later caused problems for the British.

The Bengal region had been drifting away from control by Delhi for decades. By 1740, Bengal, under Nawab Alivardi Khan, was nearly independent of Mughal rule. He died in 1756, and a struggle for power developed between his wife and his grandson. The British supported Khan's widow. This was unfortunate for the British, because the grandson Siraj Ud Daulah was victorious in the struggle for power and became the new *nawab* (ruler) of Bengal.

Siraj found the British unbearable and he decreed that Fort William be destroyed and that the British abide by the local laws. In response to Siraj's ascent to power, the British started fortifying their position at Fort William. However, in June 1756, Siraj's forces attacked and seized the fort. The British sent in more forces and retook the city of Calcutta in early 1757. Robert Clive led the British Company forces to victory. He then proceeded to conquer Siraj's forces and killed the Bengali leader only a year after he had come to power. Earlier Clive had cut a deal with Siraj's uncle, Mir Jafar, which would allow Jafar to become nawab upon the death of Siraj. In return, Clive received a huge amount of money from Jafar that instantly made him one of the richest people in Britain. British control

British major-general Robert Clive gained notoriety by conquering Bengal in the 1750s, but he also became one of the richest men in Great Britain by extracting revenue from the citizens and rulers of the provinces that the East India Company had conquered. Clive is depicted in this painting by American artist Benjamin West receiving land revenues from the provinces of Bengal, Bihar, and Orissa.

in Bengal increased and their power allowed them to extract incredible wealth from the region.

The power of the British East India Company became so great that the British government was compelled to start limiting its authority. In 1784, the East India Company Act established the authority of the British government over the company in terms of political activity. It also marked the start of the British bureaucratic system that operated in India until well into the twentieth century. In 1813, the Charter Act further asserted the authority of the British government over the lands controlled by the company.

In addition, the act ended the company's monopoly on trade, with the exception of its trade with China and its tea trade. The act also allowed Christian missionaries to enter India.

The East India Company continued to play a major role in India until a local uprising changed its role. In 1857, a number of the company's troops rebelled against British rule. This mutiny lasted nearly a year and threatened the British role on the subcontinent. The war ended with the surrender of the Indian soldiers in June 1858. Because of this uprising, the British terminated the East India Company and assumed direct control of India. By this time, the British controlled the areas that would later become the countries of India and Pakistan and, later, Bangladesh.

The direct rule by the British government brought more changes to India. English became the language of government and it was taught in schools. The civil service system and governmental bureaucracy was put into place. Transportation, education, and communication systems were all improved. Transportation and trade with the Bengal region also became important. Even with the progress made under the British government, rumblings about the need for independence were growing with the local people.

In British-held India, Muslims (followers of the Islamic faith) were in a difficult situation, because they always seemed to be less influential and less wealthy than their Hindu neighbors. As you can imagine, this bred considerable resentment. Much of the Muslims' plight, however, stemmed from the fact that they were less educated. The lower status of Muslims is well captured in a quote from Mansur Ali, a Bengali who described the situation in the following terms: "In Bengal, the landlord is Hindu, the peasant Muslim. The money lender is Hindu, the client is Muslim. The jailor is Hindu, the prisoner is Muslim. The magistrate is Hindu, the accused is Muslim." This status of inferiority was combined with a numerical disadvantage when compared to the huge Hindu population. Thus, Muslims also felt that they would be a small minority without a strong voice in an India governed by a much larger Hindu majority. This issue, based on religion and other cultural differences, would be a huge factor in the historical geography of Bangladesh during most of the twentieth century.

4

The Rise of Bangladesh

B ritish rule in India served to keep the subcontinent united as one colony for nearly the entire first half of the twentieth century. However, there were many cultural—including social, political, and religious—divisions within the subcontinent, and dissent increased throughout this period. The British fostered some of the divisions unintentionally through policies they implemented. For example, in order to establish more effective rule, in 1905 the British divided Bengal into eastern and western regions. The province called East Bengal and Assam had its capital in Dhaka, the future capital of Bangladesh. Calcutta was designated as the capital of the West Bengal province. East Bengal was more Muslim, while West was more Hindu. However, under pressure from the Hindu population, the two provinces were brought back together as a single province by the British in 1912. This caused even more concern by Muslims in East Bengal, because they saw how the blatant power of the Hindus had been used to influence the British. These concerns became a source of increasing conflict and a growing desire for independence among Muslims.

The All-India Muslim League met for the first time in Dhaka in 1906. The group had strongly supported the partitioning of East and West Bengal. The league served as a defender of Muslim interests in India and it strongly advocated Muslim political interests. In 1930, the league's president, Muhammad Iqbal, stated the need for a separate Muslim state if India became independent. Indian political leaders representing both the Hindu interests and Congress strongly opposed the idea of two states. In 1933, students came up with the name Pakistan for the proposed Muslim state.

Mohammad Ali Jinnah became the leader of the Muslim League in 1934. He extended the idea of two nations even further by explaining the religious and other cultural differences between Muslims and Hindus. On the other hand, Hindus opposed the idea of partitioning India into Muslim and Hindu sectors. It seemed that the more they opposed the idea, however, the more the Muslim population supported the notion of two countries. Many worked to bridge the growing gap between the two populations. Among these was Mohandas Gandhi, who made repeated attempts to connect the two factions. All of these efforts and others failed because the divisions had become too great.

The British House of Commons passed the Indian Independence Act on July 14, 1947. Pakistan became independent on August 14, 1947, and India became independent on August 15, 1947. Needless to say, chaos followed.

A DIVIDED PAKISTAN

Following independence, fear for the future immediately uprooted millions of Hindus who moved to lands now designated part of India. Millions of Muslims, on the other hand, fled their homes to seek safety in the lands of the new country

Mohammad Ali Jinnah (left), who is pictured here with Mohandas Gandhi at Jinnah's home in Bombay in September 1944, believed that India's Hindu and Muslim populations should each have their own states. Jinnah got his wish in August 1947, when Great Britain partitioned India into Muslim Pakistan and Hindu India.

Pakistan. Violence, rioting, persecution, genocide, and abductions ensued immediately after independence for the two new countries. An estimated 12 to 14 million people moved one way or the other, and more than half a million people died. Independence had been gained, but at what cost to countless millions of people?

The future country of Bangladesh was now referred to as East Pakistan. Pakistan was a physically divided country, with the two sections on opposite sides of the Indian subcontinent, 1,000 miles (1,600 kilometers) apart. The country's capital city, Karachi, and an estimated 90 percent of the nation's wealth were centered in West Pakistan. Meanwhile, 90 percent of the country's population lived in relatively poor and powerless East Pakistan. Political and economic decisions made by their government naturally favored West Pakistan. There were major cultural differences as well. One vitally important difference was the languages used in each region. Urdu was advocated by West Pakistan as the official language, and Bengali, the dominant language of East Pakistan, received second-class status. Most people in East Pakistan could not even understand Urdu. They were furious over the political decision made in distant Karachi to elevate Urdu to the status of the country's official tongue.

In 1952, student demonstrations in East Pakistan ended in violence when police killed two protestors. Two years later, East Pakistan was successful in pressuring the Karachi government to recognize both Bengali and Urdu as the official languages of the country. However, the seeds of division between East and West Pakistan already had been solidly planted because of the language issue.

The Muslim League became a political party after Pakistan secured its independence. However, in the 1954 elections, East Pakistan rejected the Muslim League in favor of local parties such as the Peasants and Workers Socialist Party and the Awami League (People's League). These parties formed a coalition that worked to oppose the dominance of West Pakistan. Divisions between the political parties and regional violence slowed the process of partition with West Pakistan. However, interest in an independent East Pakistan (to be called Bangladesh) grew larger each year.

Before becoming Bangladesh's first prime minister, Sheikh Mujibur Rahman headed the Awami League, which promoted greater autonomy for East Pakistan. Pictured here in 1972, Rahman would later ban all opposition political parties in Bangladesh and declare himself president for life.

New issues served to further divide East and West Pakistan. Foreign aid sent to the country was held in West Pakistan, and little trickled through to East Pakistan. In 1966, the leader of the Awami League, Sheikh Mujibur Rahman (who was usually referred to as Mujib), issued a six-point political and economic program for East Pakistan. The key idea in his agenda was to increase the autonomy of East Pakistan. President Mohammad Ayub Khan of Pakistan was trying to push the country in the opposite direction, toward integration of East and West Pakistan. Mujib was arrested by the government in 1968. Violence, strikes, and protests followed, and in

1969, Ayub resigned and General Agha Mohammad Yahya Khan assumed control of the Pakistani government. He instituted martial law to quell the chaos and violence.

Events turned unexpectedly on November 12, 1970, when a devastating cyclone hit East Pakistan. A quarter of a million people died. Two days after the cyclone, General Yahya came from Karachi to view the situation. He appeared indifferent to the problems, which enraged the people of East Pakistan. Political fissures appeared in the December elections in 1970, and West Pakistan started moving more troops into the East. The political, economic, and social fault lines between East and West had reached a breaking point. General Yahya had decided to quash East Pakistan by using the military. A crushing crackdown campaign of terror started on March 25, 1971. The following day, Bangladesh declared its independence from a radio station seized in Chittagong.

The military's purpose was to force East Pakistan to submit to the power of the central Pakistani government. They had prepared "hit lists" to eliminate leaders who were a threat in Dhaka, a city defenseless against the Pakistani Army. Hundreds died on that first night of bitter fighting. However, local people came to see this as the beginning of the war for liberation. The war took a huge toll on East Pakistan. Not only were land, infrastructure, and crops damaged or destroyed, but an estimated 1 million people died in the nine months of fighting.

Eight to 10 million refugees flooded into India from East Pakistan. This spurred the Indian Parliament into action, condemning the Pakistani military and providing support to the rebels in Bangladesh. The Indian Army proceeded to invade East Pakistan on December 4, 1971, and took the city of Dhaka. In only 12 days, the Indian Army, with the aid of Bangladeshi freedom fighters, routed Pakistani forces in Bangladesh.

The Constitution of Bangladesh was adopted on November 4, 1972. It was patterned after the Indian Constitution and created a parliamentary form of government. Mujib became prime minister, and Dhaka was designated as the capital city for the fragile new nation.

EARLY YEARS AS A NATION

After the war, Bangladesh was in shambles. Ruined cities, a devastated economy, and a population ravaged by widespread death, rape, hunger, and displacement from homes were left in the wake of conflict. Chaos, violence, and anarchy had existed in the society for years under Pakistani rule. The new government faced the daunting task of regaining civil authority and creating law and order. A major famine in 1974 made the situation even more precarious. The government estimated that 26,000 died, while some international sources claim the number was closer to 1 million.

In his efforts to solve the country's problems and the resistance that existed against his rule, Mujib became more repressive. Political parties were terminated, the media was muzzled, and personal freedoms were severely restricted. He created a one-party state with himself as president. In a coup led by young military officers, Mujib and many of his family were assassinated on August 15, 1975. This coup ushered in a 15-year period of military rule that lasted until 1990.

Major General Ziaur Rahman served as the leader of Bangladesh from 1975 to 1981. His leadership started the process of restoring law and order to the chaotic country. He also tried to establish a political party and held elections, but there were frequent attempts to assassinate him. The last attempt was successful. In May 1981, Rahman was killed in Chittagong in a coup led by Major General Manzur Ahmed.

After a short time during which the vice president led the country, Hussain Mohammed Ershad seized power in 1982. He assumed full control and declared martial law. This power grab was resented by many Bangladeshis, because the former government had been elected with the reforms established by Rahman. In contrast, Ershad was a true military dictator. During

Tens of thousands of Bangladeshis gathered in Dhaka on March 26, 2006, to celebrate the thirty-fifth anniversary of the country's independence. The national holiday is marked by parades, concerts, sporting events, and the paying of respect at the National Martyrs' Memorial, or Jatiyo Smriti Soudho, to honor those who sacrificed their lives in the name of independence.

his rule, he established Islam as the state religion and fought efforts to democratize the country. His rule ended when the army withdrew support from him and supported democratization. With popular support and the military against him, Ershad resigned in December 1990.

In early 1991, free elections were held and Khaleda Zia was selected by Parliament to be prime minister. Zia was the wife of Ziaur Rahman and has remained very popular in the country. She served until 1996 and instituted a number of reforms in education and in making the country more democratic. After she left office, Zia's opposition, led by Sheikh Hasina Wajed, took over. From 1996 to 2001, Hasina served as prime minister and worked to further the processes of good governance in the country. One major contribution was his improvement of health care. Zia returned as prime minister in 2001. New parliamentary elections are scheduled to be held in January 2007.

BANGLADESH TODAY

The legacy of Bangladesh's past is very important to Bangladeshis. On March 26, 2006, the country celebrated 35 years of independence. The celebration was marked in Dhaka with tens of thousands of people gathering to watch parades and a show of military aircraft. More than 10,000 police stood nearby important venues, because the threat of militant attacks loomed. Other cities also marked the event with celebrations as the country reflected back on the chronicles of its past and the contributions of martyrs who helped the country emerge victorious after the nine-month war of liberation from Pakistan.

The Independence Day celebration provides Bangladeshis with an opportunity to reflect back on the promises held by independence—those that have been fulfilled and those that have failed to be met. Military repression and rule by distant authorities have left scars on the country, but the roots of democracy grow deeper each year. While floods, famine, and cyclones can strike unpredictably and devastate sections of the low-lying country, the human spirit of independence and a search for freedom remain very much alive.

5

People and Culture

Have you ever seen a photograph—perhaps in a textbook, promotional literature for a foundation that attempts to address the growing global population problem, or in the media—that shows a city street with elbow-to-elbow people? Odds are it was taken in Dhaka, Bangladesh's capital and largest city. Dhaka is a "poster child" for those who are concerned about the world's large and growing human population. When thinking about Bangladesh, perhaps more so than any other country in the world, people—masses of people—come to mind. How do these people live? What is their language, their faith, and their day-to-day way of living? These are some of the topics we will consider in this chapter.

THE GRIM POPULATION STATISTICS

Data relating to the Bangladeshi population hold little room for optimism. Imagine putting nearly one-half the population of the entire

United States into an area about the size of the state of Mississippi. Things would be a bit crowded, wouldn't they! How would people find land on which to live and raise crops to feed their families? How could the government provide adequate services such as sanitation, schooling, and medical care? How could people find jobs? In order to understand the incredible population problem Bangladesh faces, we must first have an understanding of the demographic data and what they mean. (Demography is the statistical study of the human population.) Regarding the following data, however, a word of caution must be given. Sources often differ on the figures that they give. For example, the *CIA World Factbook* indicates an annual rate of natural population increase of 2.0 percent, whereas the Population Reference Bureau places the figure at 1.9 percent. Bangladesh last took an official census in 2001, but for a variety of reasons, many of the figures represent little more than educated guesses. This situation is typical of less-developed countries, in which taking a detailed national census is extremely costly.

By mid-2006, the population of Bangladesh will approach 150 million, almost exactly one-half that of the United States. Among countries, it ranks seventh in terms of population, placing it ahead of Russia, Nigeria, and Japan. For a country of its size, it has far and away the highest population density, an almost unbelievable 2,600 people per square mile (about 1,004 per square kilometer). Only a few small island states such as Singapore, Malta, and Bahrain, or micro-states such as Monaco, have a higher density. With an annual birth-rate of about 28 per 1,000 and death rate of only 8 per 1,000, rapid growth clearly is occurring and will continue to expand. In fact, with an annual growth rate of around 2 percent, the population is growing nearly twice as fast as the world average (1.15 percent). If this growth continues at the current rate, the country's population will increase to about 230 million by the year 2050. As you can see, in terms of population and crowding, things may get much worse in the future unless the country can come to grips with its runaway population growth.

As has previously been noted, Bangladesh is one of the world's poorest countries. Poverty and population often go hand in hand in terms of cause and effect. Many poor people in the less-developed world, for example, look upon children as a source of wealth. Youngsters can do chores, care for younger siblings, and certainly, as in the case of Bangladesh, hold wage-earning jobs (child labor is discussed in Chapter 7). Additionally, there is also a relationship between poverty and such conditions as increased infant mortality and decreased life expectancy. Infant mortality figures for Bangladesh are almost identical to those for the rest of the less-developed countries (LDCs). About 65 of each 1,000 newly born infants die before their first birthday. Malnutrition is a major factor in the high infant mortality. Some sources indicate that up to 50 percent of all young children go without food for one or more days each week! Life expectancy, too, is close to the average for LDCs. At birth, Bangladeshis can expect to live about 62 years, one year less than the LDC average. Males and females have comparable life expectancies, which is an anomaly. Worldwide, women typically outlive men by about five years. This difference can be explained by a very high maternal death rate, the rate of women dying when giving birth. Because of widespread poverty, sanitation is poor, and health- and medical care are scarce and financially out of reach for much of the population. Malaria, typhoid, and intestinal diseases are just some of the illnesses that take a tremendous toll each year.

A country's age structure is also important. It tells us something about patterns and trends. For example, 35 percent of all Bangladeshis are under 15 years of age (compared to 21 percent in the United States and 18 percent in Canada). This suggests that just over one-third of the population will soon be entering its reproductive years, marrying, and starting a family. In Bangladesh today, each woman gives birth to an average 3.1

One of the biggest ongoing problems in Bangladesh is malnutrition, especially among the country's youth. A number of factors contribute to this epidemic, including extreme poverty, overcrowding, and flooding, which destroys crops. Pictured here is a group of children in Dhaka waiting in line to receive food from Bangladeshi relief workers after a massive flood hit the region in August 2004.

children. This is one reason why demographers (scientists who study the human population) and population geographers are deeply concerned about the country's future. On the other hand, only 3 percent of the population is older than 65 years of age. This is below the world average of 7 percent and even the LDC average of 5 percent. This gap, too, can be explained primarily by the country's poverty.

IS BANGLADESH "OVERPOPULATED"?

Overpopulation is a widely abused, vague, and politically charged concept. In fact, it is a term that geographers and many other scientists prefer not to use. What constitutes a condition of too many people? We know, for example, that some of the world's most densely packed countries, such as Japan, rank among the very best off in terms of human well-being. People are relatively wealthy, enjoy a high standard of living, and have a long life expectancy.

At the opposite extreme, some of the world's poorest countries also rank at or near the very bottom of the world's countries in terms of low population density. People, after all, tend to cluster in places where there are jobs and where many conveniences and necessities are readily available. On the other hand, people tend to avoid those places where living is harsh and making a decent living is difficult. What all of this suggests is that population density, alone, tells us very little about whether a location is overpopulated.

Overpopulation has been defined in many ways. The following is one way of defining it: *Overpopulation is a condition reached when the human population of a defined geographic area exceeds the capacity of available land and other resources to adequately provide the essential elements of survival under existing cultural (i.e., social, political, technological, economic) and environmental conditions.* As you can see, population is but one of many variables. Available land, for example, is extremely limited in Bangladesh, as are natural resources. On the other hand, in a traditional rural, subsistence, folk culture, people need and expect much less than their urban counterparts. Most Americans and Canadians, for example, need an automobile for mobility. No such need exists for a rural villager who has never traveled beyond the neighboring village a mile or two away. In fact, in Bangladesh, only two people out of a thousand have a vehicle of their own! Social conditions, available technology and capital resources, and the effectiveness of a country's government all play an important role as well. Government, in particular, is a key to understanding whether a country's population will be able to provide for

itself adequately. As you will learn in Chapter 6, good government remains a distant dream for Bangladeshis. Considering
the data and many variables, we can safely conclude that
Bangladesh does, indeed, suffer from severe overpopulation.

SETTLEMENT

Settlement refers to where people live and how a country's population is distributed across its territory. Bangladesh is one of
the world's most rural countries, with 77 percent of its population, or about 115 of its 150 million people, living in rural environments. Few of the world's countries have a more evenly
distributed population than Bangladesh. Only in the low-lying
swamps and marshes bordering the Bay of Bengal does the
population density drop below 250 people per square mile (100
per square kilometer).

Most rural residents live in the thousands of small rural villages that crowd the countryside. Such settlements may only be
home to a hundred or so people. Life in the countryside can be
very difficult. Here, many residents continue to practice an age-
old traditional folk culture based on subsistence. People are
financially poor and generally uneducated. Rates of illiteracy
are well over 50 percent. More than half of the villages lack adequate sanitation facilities, and many do not have a supply of
pure water. Rice is the primary crop and food, and rice paddies
are a dominant feature of the cultural landscape.

Only 23 percent of the population (about 35 million people) is classified as being urban. By contrast, in most developed
countries, about 75 percent of the population is urban. Cities,
of course, are where most jobs, educational opportunities,
health- and medical facilities, and other resources are located.
The largest city, by a wide margin, is Dhaka, the capital. Various
sources list its population as being roughly 3.5 to almost 13
million—quite a range! It is extremely difficult to determine
urban populations, particularly in less-developed countries.
One problem is who and what is counted? One source, for

The capital and largest city of Bangladesh is Dhaka. Located in the central part of the country, on the Buriganga River, it is quickly becoming one of the largest cities in the world—over the last quarter of the twentieth century, the population increased by nearly 470 percent.

example, gives the population of Los Angeles, California, as "3,694,820 (16,373,645)." How is this difference explained? Los Angeles is a city (the lower figure), but the Los Angeles *metropolitan area*—the area of solid settlement that includes dozens of other cities and towns—is huge. So in the city of Dhaka proper, the lower figure of 3.5 million is no doubt close to being correct. The larger figure of 13 million refers to the metropolitan area. Think of the latter population as looking down upon a city from far above Earth's surface. You see a huge area of concentrated population, but cannot make out a city boundary. That would be the metropolitan area. If we take the higher figure for Dhaka, it would rank tenth among the world's largest urban centers. Dhaka is what geographers refer to as a *primate city*. This designation refers to an urban center that is the country's financial, political, and social and cultural center. (In contrast, the United States has no primate city, because New York City functions as its financial center and Washington, D.C., its political center.)

Chittagong, located in the southeast on the banks of the Karnaphuli River near where the stream flows into the Bay of Bengal, is the country's second-largest city. Its metropolitan area is growing rapidly, and today is home to an estimated 3.5 million people. The city, which is Bangladesh's primary seaport, is known for its cleanliness and ethnic diversity. Rajshahi, located in the northwestern part of the country, is the only other urban center with a population that approaches 1 million. It is Bangladesh's leading education center and also is known for its silk production.

Throughout much of the world over the past century, the dominant pattern of population flow has been rural to urban. When studying migration, geographers take into consideration what they call "push" and "pull" factors. Push factors are those that influence peoples' decisions to leave an area. In Bangladesh, these would include rural poverty, a lack of jobs, poor health and sanitation facilities, poor educational opportunities, few amenities, and, in general, a very difficult life. Pull factors are those that draw people toward a destination. Generally, they can be easily summarized by two factors: economic gain and a better way of life (which includes many opportunities and amenities). During recent decades, Bangladesh has experienced an upsurge in rural-to-urban migration. The country also has a migration deficit; that is, more people are moving out than moving in. Many Bangladeshis, for example, have left the country (often temporarily) to work in Middle Eastern oil fields or construction jobs.

MAJOR TRAITS OF BANGLADESHI CULTURE

This section will provide a brief overview of the major traits of Bangladeshi culture. As is true throughout much of the less-developed world, traditional lifestyles are giving way to modern living. Our discussion will begin with this transition, a concept that is critical to understanding what may be the single most significant aspect of the country's people.

The Traditional (Folk) to Contemporary (Commercial) Cultural Transition

The culture, or way of life, practiced by most Bangladeshis is in many ways similar to that found in India and elsewhere in South Asia, as well as throughout much of the less-developed world. With more than three-fourths of all Bangladeshi settlements being rural, most people are peasant farmers living in the countryside or in small farming villages. They practice a traditional folk culture, much as our ancestors did a century or more ago. In a traditional society, people are largely self-sufficient. They build their own homes, make their own clothing and other material needs, and raise their own food. In Bangladesh, rice is the major crop and dietary staple. Few people are formally educated, but this certainly does not mean that they are not smart. (Only about 20 percent of all youngsters finish high school.) In fact, they have a much better knowledge of the survival demands of day-to-day living than do most of us. We, after all, depend upon purchasing most of what we need.

In Bangladesh, as is true throughout much of the less-developed world, the old ways of living are giving way to modernization. Cities are beginning to grow rapidly, and with urban living comes cultural changes. It is very difficult, for example, to fare well within a city without a formal education, including language and mathematical literacy. City living requires a cash income and increased reliance upon others. Goods and services are purchased rather than provided by the individual. People must abide by formal laws, rather than local (often tribal) customs. There are countless other changes that must be made in order to successfully make the transition from traditional, rural, life to contemporary, commercial, urban living.

Ethnicity

Ethnicity is a very difficult term to define; in fact, within the scientific community, widespread disagreement exists in regard to its precise meaning. *Culture* can be defined as a people's way of life. *Nationality* refers to one's self-perception; if asked, "what are you?" how do you reply? Many Americans and Canadians, for example, share a very similar culture, but identify themselves as being "Americans" and "Canadians" in terms of nationality. *Ethnicity* falls somewhere in between these two terms and concepts. While most of the U.S. population identify themselves as being *American*, a Hispanic American may identify his or her ethnicity as being *Hispanic* (or any of several such terms that reflect a Latin American linkage).

The culture of most Bangladeshis is quite similar to that of many other residents of South Asia, particularly eastern India. Today, most residents of the country recognize themselves as being Bangladeshis, their national identity. Unlike many less-developed countries, including neighboring India, Bangladesh is incredibly homogeneous in regard to ethnicity. In fact, few countries in the world can claim greater ethnic "purity." Fully 98 percent of all Bangladeshis identify themselves as being Bengalis, the group for whom the country is named.

Language

Nationality, ethnicity, and language often share a common link. This is true of Bangladesh and the Bangladeshis, whose language is Bangla (also called Bengali). Nearly everyone in the country speaks this tongue, which is also the official language. Bangla is derived from the Indo-Aryan linguistic family; hence, it has close ties to Hindi (the major language of India). The language also reflects the region's cultural history, containing words from Arabic, Persian, and Turkic, as well as English. Only

More than 129 million of Bangladesh's 147 million people are Muslim, the majority of which are Sunni Muslim. Here, Muslim pilgrims pray during the final day of the three-day Islamic congregation at Tongi, Bangladesh.

a few scattered tribal groups inhabiting remote areas of the country speak their own dialect. Nearly all formally educated people also speak English, which was the colonial language.

Religion

About 83 percent of the population adheres to the Islamic faith. In fact, Bangladesh is home to the world's fourth-largest Muslim population. Only Indonesia, Pakistan, and (surprisingly, perhaps) India have more people who adhere to the

Muslim religion. Most Bangladeshis are Sunni Muslims, the denomination to which some 85 to 95 percent of the followers of the Islamic faith worldwide belong.

Most Bangladeshis are devout in their beliefs and followings as established in the holy book, the *Qur'an* (Koran). They do not eat pork or consume alcohol. Like all of the world's Muslims, they believe in the Five Pillars of Islam. The first pillar is the profession of faith, the belief in Allah, the one God whose last prophet was Mohammad. The second pillar is ritualized daily prayers, done five times each day while facing Mecca (Muslims in Bangladesh, therefore, pray toward the west). The third pillar is alms giving to the poor and needy. The fourth pillar is fasting during the holy month of *Ramadan*, the month in which the Qur'an was revealed to Mohammad (because the Islamic calendar is different from that used in the West, Ramadan falls during different seasons of the year). The fifth pillar is *hajj,* a pilgrimage to the city of Mecca in today's Saudi Arabia, where the holiest structure in Islam, the Ka'ba, or house of God, is located.

About 16 percent of the population belongs to the Hindu faith, the dominant religion of neighboring India. You will recall that East and West Pakistan broke off from the larger, Hindu-dominated India on the basis of religion. During the painful and hostile transition, millions of people died and tens of millions more were displaced. Nonetheless, today, some 24 million people of the Hindu faith live in Bangladesh. There are also a small handful of Buddhists and Christians in the country, but their numbers and cultural impact are insignificant.

Diet

Many similarities exist between the foods eaten and the ways they are prepared in Bangladesh and those found elsewhere in Southern and Southeastern Asia. As is true throughout the region, rice is the main dietary staple. Fish, poultry, and beef are too expensive for the poor, although people living along bodies of water can fish and many rural people have a small flock of chickens. Vegetables are popular, and many spices are used in preparing most dishes. Many foods are prepared in cooking oil with spices and chopped onions. Fruits, too, are consumed with nearly every meal and include mangoes, papayas, guavas, bananas, and watermelons. Rural diets are generally consistent; that is, the same foods are consumed daily and prepared in the same way. This is a dominant trait of all folk cultures. In the cities, as is true here in the United States and Canada, most people enjoy a much greater variety of foods, including those typical of foreign lands and cultures.

In this chapter, the concept of overpopulation was discussed in some detail. The level of human well-being, you will recall, is a function of many factors. A good government, which in turn contributes to a strong economy, is foundational to any nation's success. Unfortunately, as you will learn in the following two chapters, in Bangladesh, weak, ineffective, and corrupt government has contributed to widespread poverty.

6

Government and Politics

The People's Republic of Bangladesh (the country's official name) is still a very young nation. But its very long heritage and rich culture exercise a strong impact on the country's contemporary government and politics. Bangladesh's government is a parliamentary democracy. The term *democracy* comes from the Greek words *demos*, which means "the common people," and *kratein*, which means "to rule." Thus, democracy literally means the common people rule. This means that citizens have the right to democratically participate in a representative government. In Bangladesh, this is called the Jatiya Sangsad (House of the Nation). The notion of a democracy comes from the country's Indian and British legacy and the time when it was still East Pakistan. Thus, the country's various traditions have helped to shape how the country governs itself by creating a democracy that is patterned after those of India and the United Kingdom.

The structure of the Bangladesh government and its relationship to citizens is established by the country's constitution. This document, written and originally adopted in 1972, represents the highest law in the land. The constitution was suspended in 1982, when a coup led by General Hussain Mohammed Ershad toppled the government. However, the constitution was restored in 1986 and has remained in place since that time. Many changes, called amendments, have been made to the original document over time.

A number of key ideas are set forth in the preamble of Bangladesh's constitution. They serve as a declaration of core principles and as a prelude to the contents of the entire document. An abbreviated version of the preamble follows:

> We the people of Bangladesh, having proclaimed our Independence on the 26th day of March, 1971 and through a historic war for national independence, established the independent, sovereign People's Republic of Bangladesh;
>
> Pledging that the high ideals of absolute trust and faith in the Almighty Allah, nationalism, democracy and socialism meaning economic and social justice, which inspired our heroic people to dedicate themselves to, and have our brave martyrs to sacrifice their lives in the war for national independence, shall be fundamental principles of the constitution;
>
> Further pledging that it shall be a fundamental aim of the State to realize through the democratic process to socialist society, free from exploitation—a society in which the rule of law, fundamental human rights and freedom, equality and justice, political, economic and social, will be secured for all citizens;
>
> Affirming that it is our sacred duty to safeguard, protect and defend this constitution and to maintain its supremacy as the embodiment of the will of the people

of Bangladesh so that we may prosper in freedom and may make our full contribution towards international peace and co-operation in keeping with the progressive aspirations of mankind.

Some of the key indicators given by the preamble clearly show that Bangladesh is an Islamic nation. However, it is also a country with a commitment to the rule of law, equality, justice, freedom, human rights, and socialism. These ideas will be discussed in greater length later in this chapter, but their inclusion in the preamble underscores their importance to the people of Bangladesh. The preamble also reflects the importance of the struggle for independence, a difficult process that was discussed earlier in Chapter 4.

BRANCHES OF GOVERNMENT

The constitution then created the government and key processes, as well as rights and responsibilities in subsequent sections of the document. Responsibilities of the three wings of government—the executive, legislative, and judicial—also are established and defined in the constitution. A brief overview of each branch of government, including its primary characteristics and key duties, follows.

The Executive Branch

The position of the head of state that is created by the constitution is for that of the president. The president is elected by Parliament for a five-year term. The individual must be a citizen who is at least 35 years old and who is not a member of Parliament. Even though the president can be the head of the armed forces when there is a caretaker government, the position is primarily ceremonial. Caretaker governments happen when Parliament has been disbanded. This puts the president temporarily in control until a new prime minister is selected.

In 1991, Khaleda Zia became Bangladesh's first female leader when she was elected prime minister. Although she was ousted in 1996, she returned to office in 2001 and served until 2006. Zia was the wife of former president and founder of the Bangladesh Nationalist Party, Ziaur Rahman, who was assassinated in 1981.

The prime minister is the head of the government with more real political power than the president. The prime minister is responsible for the day-to-day work of the national government and for creating and implementing public policy. The president appoints the prime minister from among members of the majority political party in Parliament. The prime minister's term of office lasts as long as he/she has the support of a majority of the members of Parliament, for up to five years. All other ministers, deputy ministers, and state ministers are appointed by the prime minister. Each of the ministers is a member of the cabinet and heads up a government department in a manner much like the president's cabinet in the United States. The prime minister presides over the cabinet. The departments that are headed by ministers are mostly staffed with permanent staff, much like civil service employees in other countries. Examples of ministries in Bangladesh include Finance, Defense, Cultural Affairs, Communication, Planning, Water Resources, Agriculture, and Religious Affairs.

Bangladesh is divided politically into six regional administrative divisions—Dhaka, Chittagong, Ragshahi, Khulna, Barisal, and Sylhet. The administrative divisions assist in managing the day-to-day work of government for the executive branch. Each of these six divisions is divided into districts. There are 64 districts in the country, and these are further divided into local political entities called thanas. Bangladesh has 490 thanas. Each of these thanas is subdivided into the lowest and most local political units, which are unions and then villages.

The Legislative Branch

The legislative branch is responsible for making the national laws that govern Bangladesh. As mentioned earlier, the Jatiya Sangsad serves as the national Parliament for the country. This body was also created by the country's constitution in which it is mandated that there will be 300 members. Most of the members are directly elected by citizens from districts where only one is elected to represent the people from that area. However, with the adoption in 2004 of the Fourteenth Amendment to Bangladesh's constitution, 45 seats are now specifically reserved for women. These seats are proportionally divided among the political parties, with the House of the Nation members selecting the women. Women may also be elected to the district positions, and so there are two routes for women to become members of the Jatiya Sangsad.

Members of Parliament (MP) must be at least 25 years old and a citizen of Bangladesh. MPs serve for up to five years unless the Jatiya Sangsad is dissolved earlier by the president. Individual MPs may be removed from office for a number of reasons including incompetence, if they are convicted of a crime, or if they declare citizenship with another country.

The head offices in the Jatiya Sangsad are the speaker and deputy speaker. The speaker or the deputy speaker, in case the speaker is absent, has the responsibility of leading the sessions of Parliament. The body also has a number of standing committees that perform much of the detailed work in creating legislation for the full Jatiya Sangsad to consider.

The process of lawmaking in Bangladesh has the Jatiya Sangsad creating and considering bills for passage. Bills passed by Parliament are sent to the president for approval. The president has 15 days to consider the bill, but can send it back to the Jatiya Sangsad with a message containing suggestions for revision. If the president does not respond to the bill within the 15 days, the bill automatically becomes law. If a bill is sent back to them, the Jatiya Sangsad can either make changes or let the original bill stand. The bill then goes back, with or without changes, to the president, who this time has only seven days to approve the bill. The bill becomes law if the president approves or does not respond in seven days. The president can only approve or send back the bill, because the position does not have the power to veto pending legislation.

The Judicial Branch

The court system of Bangladesh is also patterned after the British and Indian systems. The country has both civil and criminal laws, which, combined with the constitution, make up most of the body of law in the country. However, Islamic family law is also applied though the courts, a factor that reflects the religious culture of the country. The constitution provides for an independent judiciary, which is an important element in a democratic system of checks and balances. An exception to the independent judiciary came during the military government from 1982 to 1986, when martial law courts were utilized. This changed after the constitution was reinstated in 1986. Today, the higher courts retain a strong degree of independence, but problems remain at lower court levels.

The highest court in Bangladesh is the Supreme Court. Below this are the Low Courts. Both courts may hear civil or criminal cases. Recent times have shown that the higher courts have maintained their independence, in that they have ruled against the government in a number of cases. Lower courts are a part of the executive branch and exhibit less independence due to pressure from the executive branch. This factor also has contributed to more frequent and widespread corruption in the lower courts. Since 2001, there have been efforts to separate the lower courts more from the executive branch in renewed efforts to build greater judicial independence.

Trials are public in Bangladesh and defendants have a right to counsel. Individuals have the right to appeal the decisions of lower courts. Like many democracies, the courts in Bangladesh face a large backlog of cases.

The Supreme Court is divided into the Appellate Court and the High Court. The High Court can hear cases for the first time or it can review cases from lower courts. The Appellate Court can hear appeals from all other courts, including the High Court. The rulings of the Appellate Court are final. The chief justice and other justices are appointed by the president, and justices can hold office until the age of 67. Judges can also be removed from office. Reasons for removal include mental incapacity or gross misconduct. The Supreme Judicial Council is empowered to recommend the action for removal after which the president can remove the justice from office.

THE ROLE OF CITIZENS

Citizens play the most important role in the life of a democracy. Individual rights and freedoms protected by the constitution include the following, enumerated in Part III of the document:

- Equality under the law

- Freedom from religious, caste, race, gender, or place-of-birth discrimination

- Equality of opportunity for employment

- Protection under the law

- Right to life and personal property

- Safeguards for arrest and detainment

- Prohibition of forced labor

- Freedom of movement

- Freedom of association and assembly

- Freedom of thought, conscience, and speech

- Freedom of press

- Freedom of occupation

- Freedom of religion

- Protection of home and correspondence (privacy)

- Right to own property

Under the Bangladeshi Constitution, which was ratified in 1972, citizens hold a number of rights and freedoms, including the right to vote. Here, Bangladeshi women wait in line to cast their votes in the 2001 parliamentary elections.

The duties provided in the constitution are less extensive, but do address important responsibilities of citizens. These include the duty of all citizens to observe the constitution and laws. Other responsibilities include protecting public property and performing public duties such as voting. Work is also mentioned in the constitution as both a right and duty.

DHAKA: THE GOVERNMENT'S HOME

The city of Dhaka is established as the national capital by the constitution. The city is centrally located in the country, which provides for greater citizen access to the government. Citizen access is also aided by the fact that the city is the hub for most of the country's reasonably priced public transportation systems. These include air, rail, bus, and boats plying the network of rivers that join near the city. As noted in Chapter 5, Dhaka is also the country's primate city, its financial, political, and social and cultural center.

Government buildings provide a glimpse of some of the city's interesting architecture. The Jatiya Sangsad complex is an architectural wonder that was designed by American architect Louis Kahn and built from 1964 to 1982. The old High Court building, built in 1905, presents a contrasting side of the capital reflecting a blend of European and traditional Bangladeshi architecture.

CHALLENGES FACING THE GOVERNMENT

All countries face challenges that come in a variety of forms, and Bangladesh is no exception. However, the nation and its government face greater issues than more prosperous countries or even most of its neighbors. As a poor and densely populated land, the government must address economic development and issues of poverty that are ever present and daunting in scope. The environment also presents massive challenges, with the omnipresent threat of flooding, cyclones, and tsunamis (including the aftermath of the devastating tsunami that struck in December 2004). All of these have left people homeless and struggling to get by. While international assistance helps in some of these cases, the country's government has the primary responsibility for addressing these all-too-frequent tragedies.

Other practical human challenges face the Bangladeshi government. These include a low literacy rate of only 43 percent. The literacy rate for women is even lower. Only about one in three Bangladeshi women are able to read and write, which is a major contributing factor in keeping the birthrate high. Birthrates normally decline sharply as the literacy rate of a country's women increases.

The country also has severe environmental problems. These include water and air pollution, soil erosion and degradation, widespread deforestation, and water shortages in many parts of the country. Many of these problems are becoming increasingly severe because of the country's growing population and high population density. Diseases such as bacterial diarrhea, hepatitis, typhoid fever, dengue fever, and malaria are also prevalent.

Bangladesh is a party to many international agreements that help alleviate some of the challenges the country faces. These include treaties such as the Kyoto Protocol, Hazardous Wastes, and Ozone Layer Protection agreements. International organizations such as the United Nations and the World Trade Organization also help the country to develop economically and address environmental challenges.

Even with international help, however, Bangladesh is struggling to meet its many challenges, and rampant corruption and constant political infighting deepen the problem. As noted in Chapter 1, Transparency International ranks Bangladesh as the most corrupt country in the world. Corruption permeates nearly every segment of society—political, economic, and social—and until it is curbed, the country's future is bleak. The many issues facing the government of Bangladesh remain staggering.

CHAPTER

7

Bangladesh's Economy

By nearly any measure, Bangladesh is one of the world's poorest countries. It ranks near the very bottom in nearly all measurable categories of economic well-being. These include per-capita income, gross national income purchasing power parity, and per-capita gross domestic (and national) product. The country also ranks very low in most indices that result from poverty, such as life expectancy, literacy, and energy consumption.

Before launching into a detailed discussion of the country's economic situation, one extremely important point must be made: We are measuring *their* economic condition using *our* criteria. With two-thirds of its people living in rural environments, Bangladesh remains very much a traditional society practicing what geographers call a "folk" culture. By definition, the people are nonliterate, practice a noncommercial (barter) economy, and are highly self-sufficient. Their horizons are local. Each family provides for its own needs. Parents and children may work 15 hours a day, but not one minute of their effort contributes to those indices of "well-being" (such as income) that are used in the West. What this means is that a family with no cash income whatsoever can, in terms of local values and living standards, be the "richest" family in a village. This is a very difficult concept for those of us living in a postindustrial, commercially oriented, and urban society to understand. Grasping this concept is essential if we are to understand that roughly 50 percent of the world's population continues to live in rural environments and practice a folk culture.

OVERVIEW OF THE COUNTRY'S ECONOMIC PLIGHT

The Bangladeshi economy is marked by extreme poverty and is wracked by the country's frequent political upheavals. Upon independence from Britain, an estimated 20 million people were displaced, with Muslims moving from India and flooding into Bangladesh. This in-migration left the country with an acute shortage of housing, medical support, and food. Although this migration occurred more than three decades ago, the country is still reeling from the huge influx of people. (Imagine the entire population of New York State moving to Iowa within a period of a year or two.)

But these issues are just the beginning of the country's economic problems. Floods, cyclones, and tsunamis sap its capital resources. Repeated crop failures result in frequent famines that affect millions of people. Political corruption and political infighting weaken the government's ability to fulfill its potential in guiding development. Rapid population growth often outstrips annual economic gain. The country's high population density removes potentially productive land from agricultural use. Environmental pollution is a huge problem, and one that is very costly to solve. Power is inadequate, even as the country has one of the world's lowest per-capita uses of energy. (Energy consumption is perhaps the single most valid measure of economic growth and development.) These are just a few of the economic limitations that Bangladesh faces.

Some of these economic challenges are staggering. The average gross national income purchasing power parity (GNI-PPP) per person in 2005 was only $2,100 per year. (The GNI-PPP refers to the amount of goods and services one could buy in the United States with, in the case of Bangladesh, an annual income of $2,100.) The Population Reference Bureau (PRB) states that 83 percent of the population lives on less than $2.00 a day, and 45 percent of the population falls below the poverty line. Almost unbelievably, PRB data show that nearly one-third of all Bangladeshis (29 percent) live on less than $1.00 a day! The consequences of this widespread poverty exist on every street corner, reach into every rural settlement and agricultural field, and permeate every segment of society. Poverty creates a huge barrier that severely limits the hopes and dreams of the country and its people to get ahead economically.

One of the consequences of this poverty is that families often require their children to work in order to help the family survive. Let's bring this issue closer to home. Some article of clothing that you are now wearing may have been manufactured by a child laborer in Bangladesh. She (in most cases) may earn a dollar or two a day for working a 12-hour shift, 7 days a week, and in an unsafe environment. OneWorld South Asia, an organization seeking to bring about a more fair and sustainable world, estimates that 7 to 8 million children are working in the country. Many of these youngsters are employed in extremely hazardous jobs, ranging from construction workers, to stone crushers, to prostitutes. OWSA estimates that 20 percent of the workers in Bangladesh are children.

The issue of child labor in Bangladesh has drawn the concern and aid of the international community. Working children also are not attending school, a factor adding to the country's grossly substandard literacy rate. Lacking a formal education, these youngsters become locked in to a life of illiteracy and poverty, a factor that threatens both the children's future and that of the country. To address this complex issue, governmental and nongovernmental organizations (NGOs) alike are working in the country to reduce the tragedy of child labor. Unfortunately, in such an impoverished country, their success has been very limited.

With the difficulties facing economic development in Bangladesh, it is important that we also examine other facets of the economy. The following topics focus upon the different sectors of Bangladesh's economy. It spotlights the economic problems and potentials that exist within the country.

AGRICULTURE

Farming in Bangladesh is a very challenging occupation. Most farmers work on a very small plot of land with perhaps a few animals supplementing the growing of various crops. There is little machinery, because equipment is expensive and human labor is cheap. Adding labor-saving machinery would drastically increase unemployment. Thus, efforts to increase production by using more tractors and other machines may not be a desirable solution for this country's struggling economy.

Agriculture is by far the leading occupation for the people of Bangladesh. Nearly two-thirds of the workforce is engaged in agriculture. However, agriculture only provides one-fifth of the country's gross domestic product (GDP). (GDP is a measure of the total value of goods and services produced within a country during a one-year period.) Bangladesh's Ministry of Agriculture reports that 71 percent of all agricultural production comes from growing crops, 9 percent from raising livestock, and 10 percent each from forestry and fishing. Despite the country's economic emphasis on agriculture, Bangladesh still needs to import huge quantities of food in order to feed its population.

Fortunately, Bangladesh is blessed with fertile lands. Rice is of major importance as a food product to the Bangladeshis.

Rice is Bangladesh's primary agricultural crop and a staple of the people's diet. Here, Bangladeshi women plow rice at a rice mill in Dhamrai, which is 25 miles (40 kilometers) from the capital of Dhaka.

Grains such as wheat also have become increasingly important in the Bangladeshi diet. Other major crops include jute (a fiber), tea, and tobacco. Bangladesh is the world's leading producer of jute, which is used to make threads that can be woven into cloth, sacks, carpet, mats, rope, and many other products. Sugarcane, potatoes, and various tropical fruits also are raised, as are oilseeds, spices, and peas, beans, and lentils (crops collectively called pulses). Pulses are becoming more important in Bangladesh's efforts to feed its people.

Even though livestock plays some role in the economy, this agricultural sector suffers from a low quality of animal stock. Cattle, water buffalo, sheep, goats, and poultry are the primary animals raised in Bangladesh. Fishing is also a contributor to the diet and economy, and most fishing is done by using weighted throw nets. Forestry also adds to the country's agricultural production, with most of the wood used for the production of pulp and paper.

MANUFACTURING

During recent decades, manufacturing has shown considerable growth in Bangladesh, because labor is so cheap. Slightly more than one of every four jobs (about 27 percent) are in the country's manufacturing sector. Low labor costs lure many foreign manufacturers to the country. In fact, a number of U.S. companies have outsourced low-skill jobs to Bangladesh and elsewhere in southern and eastern Asia. This practice is criticized by some Americans, but in reality it is a "win-win" practice. First, Bangladeshis are able to work in wage-paying jobs. As their cash income grows, their level of living rises and they are able to purchase more products, including those made in the United States. Second, because wages are much lower than those paid in the United States, savings are passed on to the purchaser/consumer.

Most manufacturing is related to processing, the production of such things as cotton textiles, jute, tea, paper and newsprint, cement, chemical fertilizer, and sugar. Industrial production is increasing at a rate of about 7 percent per year. The garment and clothing industries are of particular importance, accounting for nearly 4,000 factories, most of which are located near Dhaka. In 2005, the PBS television program *Frontline* reported manufactured clothing and other garments make up 75 percent of the country's exports. The program also indicated that 38 percent of the country's garment exports are sent to the United States.

Foreign investment is encouraged in Bangladesh. With the exception of companies that play a role in the country's national security (such as currency printing, arms, and ammunition), firms can be 100 percent foreign owned. Other factors encouraging foreign investment in Bangladesh include cheap rent and low taxes. Additionally, English is the language of business and also is widely spoken and understood by many citizens.

Potential foreign investors also face problems. Difficulties arise with the near-universal practices of corruption and of a court system that operates very slowly. Corruption within the bureaucracy is widespread. In fact, the World Bank estimates that 2 to 3 percent of the country's GDP is stolen each year! The government customs is a place where officials often place "fees" upon goods being imported by investors. In an attempt to at least give the impression that it is doing something to solve this problem, the Bangladeshi government created an anticorruption commission in 2004. Other problems for foreign investors include low worker productivity, poor working conditions, the widespread use of child labor, and occasional threats of violence by trade unions. All of these factors add to the difficulty of making foreign investments in Bangladesh, despite the attraction of cheap labor.

The controversies over child labor, poor working conditions, and low wages have kept many companies out of the country. Some businesses, in fact, have taken a corporate stance against these repressive practices. But the practices also must be placed within the context of the cultural system of which they are a part. Oppressive child labor practices and dangerous working conditions, of course, cannot be justified under any condition. But keep in mind that these children are working to help their families financially. "Bad" working environments are commonplace throughout all but the developed world. Our definition of bad, and theirs, are often far apart. For example, we might demand an air-conditioned workplace, whereas those living in the country are used to the heat and humidity. Finally, you must remember that income is relative. In Bangladesh, a person who works for just a fraction of our wages, and well below our "poverty level," may, in fact, be very wealthy by local standards.

TRADE

Bangladesh is also connected to the global economy through trade. In fact, the only way any less-developed country can progress economically is by accepting and participating in the process of globalization. Because of low labor costs, Bangladesh can produce manufactured goods more cheaply than in countries where labor is more expensive. Chief among Bangladesh's exports are clothing, jute, leather, and seafood. Imports include machinery and equipment, chemicals, iron and steel, textiles, foodstuffs, petroleum products, and cement. The country still imports more than it exports, and this trade deficit adds to the country's debt and poverty.

Forty-one percent of the country's products go to other nations. The main markets for Bangladesh's exports are developed countries such as the United States (24.2 percent), Germany (13.2 percent), United Kingdom (10.6 percent), France (6 percent), and Italy (4 percent). Imports come primarily from China (18.7 percent), India (14.7 percent), Kuwait (8 percent), Singapore (6 percent), and Japan (4.4 percent).

COMMUNICATION

Communication systems are still somewhat limited in Bangladesh, a situation that is not surprising, considering the high degree of poverty in the country. For example, with a population of more than 147 million people, there are 1,007,000 land phone lines. Adding an estimated 9 million cell phones in use today, there is still only about 1 phone for every 15 people. The Internet is still in its infancy, having only arrived in Bangladesh in 1996. In the entire country, there is only one Internet host company and barely more than 300,000 Internet users. In stark contrast, with twice the population, the United States has more than 115 million Internet host companies and more than 160 million users. The Internet country code for Bangladesh is .bd.

Television and radio also are limited in Bangladesh. There are only 15 television broadcast stations and 24 radio stations. Included in the radio stations are 12 FM and 12 AM stations. Televisions are 2½ times more likely to be owned by urban families than rural. In fact, electricity is only available to about one-fourth of all rural citizens. Radio (which can be battery operated) is more common in rural areas as a means of receiving news and entertainment programs. Satellites are making more channels available, and many older Western series are available. Television programs from India are also popular in Bangladesh. Shows like *Who Wants to be a Millionaire?* have been imported from India and are well received by the viewers in Bangladesh. Other shows have a local flavor and are much more like soap operas. These include shows like *Sporsher Baire, Tin Purush,* and *Shabuj Chhaya,* a drama about village life. Programs like Shabuj Chhaya are also very useful in teaching about important health topics such as family planning and AIDS.

The country also has a number of newspapers that are published in English, Bengali, and other local languages (with Bangla dominating the local tongues). The *Daily Star* is the largest English newspaper in the country. Censorship has declined, but the government still has power, because it pays to place advertisements in newspapers, and this can influence editors to be favorable to the government.

TRANSPORTATION FACILITIES

Extensive poverty in Bangladesh limits ownership of private vehicles for almost all citizens. In fact, according to government data, there are only about 2 vehicles per 1,000 people. Obviously, this suggests that people don't get around in their private car; rather, they stay home or rely on public transportation. In a folk culture, few people ever travel beyond the horizon that they could see at birth. In fact, most of the world's people rarely travel beyond their immediate village and neighborhood!

Public transportation in Bangladesh can be a startling and colorful affair, with a ride serving as an unforgettable journey for visitors. Buses made out of wood and human-powered tricycle rickshaws are just two of the fascinating means of public

Getting around the capital city of Dhaka is often an adventure, because the streets are overcrowded and public transportation is unreliable. One of the most popular forms of transportation is the rickshaw, a two-wheeled vehicle pulled by people. In Dhaka, which is pictured here, as many as 400,000 people are employed as rickshaw-pullers.

transportation. If the bus gets filled by passengers, don't worry; riders will climb on to the roof to get a ride. However, public transportation can be quite an adventure for road passengers. Buses and other vehicles are poorly maintained and frequently break down. Considering the small number of vehicles on the road, there are an amazing number of accidents.

Other means of transportation include trains, riverboats, and planes. Using these means of travel also can be quite an adventure for the traveler. Trains have three different gauges of track, resulting in frequent changes from train to train. Another problem with trains is that they are quite slow. Not only are tracks often in poor condition, but few railroad bridges cross rivers. Passengers must be ferried across rivers. With all their problems, trains are, however, usually safer and more dependable than buses. The country has 15 paved airports and one unpaved runway. Dhaka is the hub for both the rail and air transportation systems, and also the key air link to international destinations.

Dhaka links the country to Europe, Asia, and many other destinations with a number of international airlines that serve Zia International Airport. Among these are British Airways, Air France, Iran Air, Air India, KLM, Singapore Airlines, Malaysia Airlines, Dragon Air, and Thai International. Domestic air service is provided by the government-owned Biman and privately owned GMG Airlines. These carriers mostly fly from Dhaka to key cities like Chittagong, Barisal, Jessore, Rajshahi, and Saidpur.

Water transportation is very important to the country, and includes both private and government operations. Some forms are ferries that assist people in crossing waterways that are not spanned by bridges. Others run up and down rivers and other waterways providing affordable long-distance transportation for people and products. Adventuresome water travelers can take the *Rocket*. This is a generic term given to special boats that run daily between Khulna and Dhaka with frequent stops along the way. The reason the trip can be an adventure is that the rockets have frequent accidents, including many in which people have lost their lives. Yet, because of the low prices for tickets, the boats are popular with locals, and each year more than 20 million people ride the rocket.

Seemingly, there is little room for optimism when judging the future of the Bangladeshi economy. Yet, there is some room for hope. In the following chapter, we will gaze into a hypothetical crystal ball and attempt to see what the future holds for this fragile land and troubled people.

CHAPTER 8

Bangladesh Looks Ahead

When attempting to look ahead to the future of Bangladesh, it is difficult to be optimistic. Few countries in the world have had a more turbulent past, are confronted with more problems today, or have more barriers to a better future. Environmental hazards, political instability, corruption, a dominantly rural folk society, and poorly developed infrastructure are just some of the conditions that lock the country into a perpetual cycle of poverty and frustration. In this final chapter, we will review each of the primary topics covered in this book and assess their role in guiding the country's future.

The natural environment is not going to change, at least on a large scale. Floods from the country's rivers and storms from the Bay of Bengal will continue to batter the country and its people. As the population continues to grow, more and more people will be forced to move into hazard zones such as river floodplains and the low-lying coast. As this occurs, destruction of property and loss of life will

As the population of Bangladesh continues to grow, more and more people will be forced to move to flood-prone areas. Although temporary measures such as reinforcing the riverbanks with concrete slabs can help in the short term, Bangladeshis will have to come up with a better way to warn citizens of impending floods.

accelerate. During the mid-1990s, the government took steps to improve the early storm warning system in the coastal zone, and this will help somewhat. It is impossible, however, to cover all settled areas. Upstream on the major rivers, deforestation continues in the upper elevations of their drainage basins. This, too, will increase the threat of downstream flooding. Little can be done to change this pattern. Looking ahead at possible long-term environmental change there looms the threat of global sea level rise due to apparent rising global temperatures. Whereas this potential damage is still decades away, even a rise of several feet (one meter) would be incredibly destructive to low-lying Bangladesh. Some scientists also believe that warming temperatures will contribute to more frequent and powerful cyclones. This, too, would have a devastating effect on much of the country.

History has been both kind and cruel to Bangladesh. Geographer Erhard Rostlund once noted that "the present is the fruit of the past and contains the seeds of the future." Applied to Bangladesh, this suggests that past history may provide a glimpse of the future. Can we really expect major changes in those social, political, and economic conditions that have plagued the country since its beginning?

Culturally, Bangladesh is relatively homogeneous in such key categories as ethnicity, language, religion, and general day-to-day life. This provides a sturdy foundation upon which to build a strong sense of national identity and of a unified people. Problems attributed to cultural diversity are evident in many places around the world—the former USSR the former Yugoslavia, many areas of Africa, and even parts of Canada. At least Bangladesh appears to be in a position to skirt this potential source of conflict.

There is one cultural reality that is going to be at the forefront in Bangladesh for decades to come. That is the continuing transition from a dominantly rural, traditional, self-sufficient folk culture to a commercial, specialized, urban culture with increasing global influences. In North America a century ago, many Americans and Canadians lived a day-to-day folk culture existence. By the mid-1900s, this way of life was rapidly vanishing and was found only in remote areas such as the Arctic, upland areas including Appalachia and the Ozarks, parts of the rural Deep South, and the Spanish Southwest. The United States and Canada, in undergoing the transition from traditional to contemporary culture, were countries that had a wealth of resources, a strong economy, and good government. Bangladesh is making this cultural leap, but without strong support from key institutions.

Population figures have been presented in several contexts throughout this book. When you picture Bangladesh, imagine

The literacy rate in Bangladesh is around 40 percent, but in recent years, the government has instituted a number of programs that promote reading and writing. Pictured here is a Bangladeshi teacher giving lessons to children who live in the fishing village of Shyamnagar, southwest of Dhaka.

one-half the population of the entire United States crammed into an area about the size of Iowa or Wisconsin! This image gives you a good idea of what, no doubt, is the country's chief problem—people. Yet if we look back only 10 years, the country's population was growing at the explosive rate of 2.9 percent per year. Today, it is estimated to be 1.9 percent, a drop of a full percent. This decline, perhaps more than any other fact, provides a cause for optimism concerning the country's future. If Bangladesh is going to improve, it is imperative that annual economic gain outstrip population growth. For the first time in the country's history, this is beginning to occur.

Politically, Bangladesh is now in its fourth decade of self-government. It has held free elections since 1990. With the global community (and its relatively stable and much larger neighbor, India) looking on with a critical eye, there is a glimmer of hope that the country will become even more politically stable. If this is to occur, however, it is absolutely imperative that politicians and government be open and honest in their dealings. The country must crack down, and crack down very hard, on rampant corruption. Corruption permeates every segment of the country's service sector, government, and economy. Along with cumbersome bureaucratic red tape, it discourages economic investment within the country. With only about 40 percent of the population able to read and write, illiteracy is also a staggering barrier to overcome. Building a literate society is an extremely important issue, as educated workers are much more in demand by foreign investors.

The economic challenges facing Bangladesh are truly daunting. The country is beset by numerous human challenges and also by a host of natural disasters that frequently strike the country. Yet there is cause for hope. At a smaller level, some families are finding hope in microcredit loans, small loans made available by some organizations and agencies that are used for income-generating self-employment activities. A microcredit-created business can make a tremendous differ-ence for a poor family. Organizations such as the World Bank provide the funds for these loans, which are usually less than $100. But they provide many Bangladeshis with the impetus for personal economic development. There are other reasons for optimism. For example, it is estimated that the country's textile exports will double to $15 billion a year by 2011. Other efforts also exist, but huge challenges remain for Bangladesh. Ulti-mately, as is true of most less-developed countries, the future of Bangladesh rests squarely in the hands of the country's govern-ment and its people.

Physical Geography

Location   Subcontinent of (South) Asia; bordered on three sides by India (2,518 miles, 4,053 kilometers) and by Myanmar in the southeast (120 miles, 193 kilometers); borders the Bay of Bengal to the south (360 miles, 580 kilometers)

Area   Total: 55,599 square miles (144,000 square kilometers); land: 51,703 miles (133,910 square kilometers); water: 3,896 miles (10,090 square kilometers); slightly smaller than Iowa

Climate   Monsoon tropical; mild winter (October to March); hot, humid summer (March to June); humid, warm rainy monsoon (June to October)

Terrain   Mostly flat, low-lying alluvial plain; hilly in southeast

Water Features   Most of the country is situated on deltas of large rivers flowing from the Himalayas: the Ganges unites with the Jamuna (main channel of the Brahmaputra) and later joins the Meghna to eventually empty into the Bay of Bengal

Elevation Extremes   Lowest point is the Indian Ocean (sea level); highest point is Keokradong, 4,035 feet (1,230 meters)

Land Use   Arable land, 55.39%; permanent crops, 3.08%; other, 41.53% (2005)

Irrigated Land   18,244 square miles (47,250 square kilometers) (2003)

Natural Hazards   Floodwater covers much of the country during the summer months, resulting in river flooding, coastal storm-surge flooding from Bay of Bengal during storms, and high water resulting from heavy monsoon precipitation; droughts during eight-month dry season; cyclones

Environmental Issues   Many people live on and cultivate flood-prone land; widespread disease related to pollution and insects; widespread air- and water (coastal, fresh surface, and ground) pollution; soil erosion and degradation; deforestation; threat of rising global sea level

People

Population   147,365,352 (July 2006 est.); males, 75,552,349 (2006 est.); females, 71,813,003 (2006 est.)

Population Density	2,600 per square mile (1,004 per square kilometer)
Population Growth Rate	2.0% (2006 est.)
Net Migration Rate	-0.68 migrant(s)/1,000 population (2006 est.)
Fertility Rate	3.11 children born/woman (2006 est.)
Life Expectancy at Birth	Total population: 62.5 years; male, 62.47 years; female, 62.45 years (2006 est.)
Median Age	22.2 years; male, 22.2 years; female, 22.2 years (2006 est.)
Ethnic Groups	Bengali, 98%, tribal groups and others, 2 percent
Religions	Muslim, 83%, Hindu, 16%, other, 1%
Languages	Bangla (official, also known as Bengali), English
Literacy	(age 15 and over can read and write) Total population: Estimated to be 43% (male, 54%; female, 32%) (2003 est.)

Economy

Currency	Taka; 69.7 taka per U.S. dollar (August 2006)
GDP Purchasing Power Parity (PPP)	$304 billion (2005 est.)
GDP Per Capita (PPP)	$2,100 (2005 est.)
Labor Force	67 million
Unemployment	N/A
Labor Force by Occupation	Agriculture, 63%; industry, 26%; services, 11%
Agricultural products	Rice, jute, tea, wheat, sugarcane, potatoes, tobacco, pulses, oilseeds, spices, fruit, beef, milk, poultry
Industries	Cotton textiles, jute, garments, tea processing, paper newsprint, cement, chemical fertilizer, light engineering, sugar
Exports	$9.372 billion (2004 est.)
Imports	$12.97 billion (2004 est.)
Leading Trade Partners	Exports: U.S., 24.2%; Germany, 13.2%; U.K., 10.6%; France, 6% (2004). Imports: China, 18.7% (including Hong Kong); India, 14.7%; Kuwait, 8%; Singapore, 6%; Japan, 4.4% (2004)
Export Commodities	Garments, jute and jute goods, leather, frozen fish and other seafood
Import Commodities	Machinery and equipment, chemicals, iron and steel, textiles, foodstuffs, petroleum products, cement

| **Transportation** | Roadways: 148,648 miles (239,226 kilometers), of which 14,121 miles (22,726 kilometers) are paved (2003); Airports: 16–15 are paved runways (2006); Waterways: 5,202 miles (8,372 kilometers), with distance reduced by about one-third during dry season |

Government

Country Name	Conventional long form: People's Republic of Bangladesh; Conventional short form: Bangladesh; Local long form: Gana Prajatantri Banladesh; Local short form: Banladesh; Former: East Bengal, East Pakistan
Capital City	Dhaka
Type of Government	Parliamentary democracy
Head of Government	Prime Minister Khaleda Zia (since October 10, 2001)
Independence	March 26, 1971 (from West Pakistan); December 16, 1971 (creation of the official state of Bangladesh)
Administrative Divisions	Six divisions: Barisal, Chittagong, Dhaka, Khulna, Rajshahi, and Sylhet

Communications

TV stations	15 (1999)
Phones	(Line) 1,007,000; (cell) 9,000,000
Internet Users	300,000 (2005)

* Source: CIA-The World Factbook (2006)

1,000 B.C.	Dravidians arrive in the area of Bengal now called Bangladesh.
321	Mauryan Empire begins with Chandragupta Maurya.
296	Chandragupta Maurya dies.
273	Ashoka Maurya is born.
232	Ashoka dies.
180	End of Mauryan Empire.
A.D. 319	Beginning of Gupta and Samatata empires.
335	Chandragupta I dies and Samudragupta becomes the king of Gupta Empire.
380	Samudragupta dies and Chandragupta II becomes king of Gupta Empire, which reaches its golden age during the rule of Samudragupta.
413	Chandragupta II dies.
480	White Huns (Hephthalites) invade Gupta Empire from Central Asia.
500	Hephthalites control most of the Gupta Empire.
670	Shashanka, Bengal's first independent king, dies.
750	Gopala becomes king of Bengal region, start of the Pala Dynasty.
1097	Senas begin their rise to power.
1150	End of the Pala Dynasty.
1202	Turks arrive from Turkmenistan to take control of Bengal region.
1227	Turk leadership in Bengal forced to accept Delhi Sultanate's authority.
1341	Bengal becomes independent of Delhi's authority.
1537	Portuguese establish a colony in Hughli in Bengal region.
1556	Akbar the Great comes to power in Delhi, greatly expanding the Mughal Empire, which had been established in 1526.
1576	Akbar the Great conquers Dhaka.
1600	British East India Company established in a charter by Queen Elizabeth I.
1605	Akbar dies.

1625	Dutch establish a settlement in Chinsura.
1658	British take control of Portuguese colony in Hughli.
1675	French establish a settlement in Chandernagar; Danes establish a settlement in Serampore.
1690	British establish a settlement in Calcutta.
1698	East India Company chartered to compete with the British East India Company.
1699	Fort William built in Calcutta by British East India Company.
1702	British East India Company and East India Company merge.
1756	Forces of Siraj Ud Daulah attack Fort William.
1757	British retake Fort William and kill Siraj Ud Daulah; end of the Mughal Empire.
1784	British Parliament passes the East India Company Act.
1813	Charter Act passed by British Parliament, further asserting the authority of the British government.
1905	British divide Bengal into East and West administrative regions; East Bengal capital established in Dhaka.
1906	All-India Muslim League meets for first time in Dhaka.
1912	East and West Bengal brought back together under British administration.
1930	Muhammad Iqbal states the need for a separate Muslim state.
1933	Pakistan is suggested as a name for the new Muslim state.
1947	British pass the India Independence Act; Pakistan becomes independent; India becomes independent; thousands die as millions migrate.
1966	Sheikh Mujibur Rahman (Mujib) issues a six-point program for East Pakistan.
1968	Mujib arrested in Dhaka by Pakistan government.
1969	Demonstrations, strikes, and violence cause political problems; General Agha Mohammad Yahya Khan assumes control of Pakistan's government.
1970	Devastating cyclone hits East Pakistan; West Pakistan increases troops in East Pakistan.

1971	Bangladesh declares independence from West Pakistan; India condemns military action of West Pakistan; mass exodus of 8 to 10 million immigrants to India from Bangladesh.
1972	Constitution of Bangladesh adopted.
1974	Famine kills nearly 1 million Bangladeshis.
1975	Mujib assassinated in a military coup; Major General Ziaur Rahman assumes power.
1981	Rahman assassinated in a coup led by Major General Manzur Ahmed.
1982	Hussein Mohammed Ershad seizes power and suspends the constitution.
1986	The constitution is reinstated.
1990	Ershad resigns.
1991	Free elections held and Khaleda Zia becomes prime minister.
1996	Elections held and Sheikh Hasina Wajed becomes prime minister.
2001	Khaleda Zia becomes prime minister again.
2004	Constitution amended to provide for 45 women members of Jatiya Sangsad; devastating tsunami strikes Bangladesh coast.
2006	Parliamentary elections held.

Aminul Islam, A. K. M. *A Bangladesh Village: Conflict and Cohesion.* Cambridge, Mass.: Schenkman Publishing, 1974.

Bangladesh. Ann Arbor, Mich.: CultureGrams, annual editions.

Benhart, John E., and George M. Pomeroy. *South Asia.* Philadelphia: Chelsea House Publishers, 2005.

Spencer, J. E. *Asia East by South: A Cultural Geography.* New York: John Wiley & Sons, 1954.

Further Reading

Baxter, Craig. *Bangladesh: From a Nation to a State.* Boulder, Colo.: Westview Press, 1997.

Hartmann, Betsy, and James Boyce. *Needless Hunger: Voices from Bangladesh Village.* Oakland, Calif.: Food First, 1979.

Ryan, Paul Ryder. *Bangladesh 2000: On the Brink of Civil War.* Cummington, Mass.: Munewata Press, 2000.

Web sites

Bangla2000
http://www.bangla2000.com/Bangladesh

Bangladesh Embassy, Washington, D.C.
http://www.bangladoot.org/

Bangladesh (CIA World Factbook)
https://www.cia.gov/cia/publications/factbook/geos/bg.html

A Country Study—Bangladesh (The Library of Congress)
http://lcweb2.loc.gov/frd/cs/bdtoc.html

NationMaster
http://www.nationmaster.com/country/bg-bangladesh

Population Reference Bureau, 2006 World Population Data Sheet
http://www.prb.org/pdf06/06WorldDataSheet.pdf

Wikipedia, The Free Encyclopedia
http://en.wikipedia.org/wiki/Bangladesh

The World Bank
http://www.worldbank.org

Index

Index

Picture Credits

page:

12: © Lucidity Information Design, LLC
14: Associated Press, AP
18: © Lucidity Information Design, LLC
21: Associated Press, AP
24: Associated Press, AP
31: © SEF/Art Resource, NY
36: © Time Life Pictures/Getty Images
39: © HIP/Art Resource, NY
44: Associated Press, AP
46: Associated Press, AP

49: Associated Press, AP
54: Associated Press, AP
57: © Getty Images
61: Associated Press, AP
67: ©AFP/Getty Images
72: REUTERS/Mohammad Shahidullah
79: Rafiqur Rahman/Reuters/Landov
84: Rafiqur Rahman/Reuters/Landov
88: REUTERS
90: REUTERS/Rafiqur Rahman

Cover: © 2006 Digital Vision/PunchStock

DOUGLAS A. PHILLIPS is an educator, writer, and consultant who has worked and traveled in more than 100 countries on six continents. During his career, he has worked as a middle school teacher, curriculum developer, author, and trainer of educators in many countries around the world. He has served as the president of the National Council for Geographic Education, and he has received the Outstanding Service Award from the National Council for the Social Studies, along with numerous other awards. He, his wife, Marlene, and their three children—Chris, Angela, and Daniel—have lived in South Dakota and Alaska, but now, in semiretirement, he and his wife and two sons reside in Arizona, where he writes and serves as an educational consultant for the Center for Civic Education. He has traveled throughout much of South Asia, which has given him some understanding of and a great appreciation for the region's fascinating physical environment, cultural practices, and distinctive landscapes.

CHARLES F. GRITZNER is distinguished professor of geography at South Dakota State University in Brookings. He is now in his fifth decade of college teaching, research, and writing. In addition to teaching, he enjoys writing, working with teachers, and sharing his love of geography with readers. As the series editor for Chelsea House's MODERN WORLD NATIONS (and other) series, he has had a wonderful opportunity to combine these interests. Gritzner has served as both president and executive director of the National Council for Geographic Education. He also has received many national honors, including the George J. Miller Award for Distinguished Service to Geographic Education from the NCGE and both the Distinguished Teaching Achievement Award and the Gilbert Grosvenor Honors in Geographic Education from the Association of American Geographers.